Cochrane
Marigold Library System

MAY -- 2016

FIFTY PERCENT OF
MOUNTAINEERING
IS UPHILL

D0744898

SUSANNA PFISTERER

50 PERCENT of Mountaineering is UPHILL

THE LIFE OF CANADIAN MOUNTAIN RESCUE PIONEER WILLI PFISTERER

NeWest Press

COPYRIGHT © SUSANNA PFISTERER 2016

All rights reserved. The use of any part of this publication — reproduced, transmitted in any form or by any means, electronic, mechanical, recording or otherwise, or stored in a retrieval system — without the prior consent of the publisher is an infringement of the copyright law. In the case of photo-copying or other reprographic copying of the material, a licence must be obtained from Access Copyright before proceeding.

Library and Archives Canada Cataloguing in Publication

Pfisterer, Susanna, 1962–, author
Fifty percent of mountaineering is uphill : the life of Canadian mountain rescue pioneer Willi Pfisterer / Susanna Pfisterer.

Issued in print and electronic formats.
ISBN 978-1-926455-60-0 (paperback)
ISBN 978-1-926455-61-7 (epub)
ISBN 978-1-926455-62-4 (mobi)

1. Pfisterer, Willi.   2. Mountaineers — Canada — Biography.   I. Title.

GV199.92.P45P45 2016   796.522092   C2015-906556-9   C2015-906557-7

Editor: Anne Nothof
Book design: Natalie Olsen, Kisscut Design
Author photo: Gerry Israelson

NeWest Press acknowledges the support of the Canada Council for the Arts the Alberta Foundation for the Arts, and the Edmonton Arts Council for support of our publishing program. This project is funded in part by the Government of Canada.

#201, 8540 – 109 Street
Edmonton, Alberta T6G 1E6
780.432.9427
NeWest Press www.newestpress.com

No bison were harmed in the making of this book.
Printed and bound in Canada
1 2 3 4 5   17 16 15

To Anni and Fred.

SIDEHILLGOUGER: a North American folkloric creature adapted to living on hillsides by having legs on one side of its body shorter than the legs on the opposite side.

Mount Hochkonig
overlooking
Muhlbach.

1

THE SIDEHILLGOUGER SAYS,

"Climbing a mountain is simple. Just put one foot

in front of the other and repeat."

MY MOUNTAINEERING CAREER began with an accident when I was ten years old.

Our family home in those days stood at the upper edge of a small mountain village named Muhlbach, in the Austrian Alps. The house was built on a hillside; a typical alpine-style wood structure, three stories high with a steep pitched roof and every window clustered with flowers. There was a tray of flowers at the bottom, another halfway up, and some pots hanging out to the side of each window. Those colourful blossoms were the pride and joy of my grandmother.

Like many of the other houses in the village, the outside of our home was covered with forester shingles. Each of these shingles measured ten centimetres in width, twenty centimetres in length, and were rounded at the bottom. It literally took thousands of the damn things to cover a wall. My grandfather, a seasoned mountain guide, manufactured and sold them when he was not out climbing, and I, over and above my normal chores, had to carefully pile all that he produced along one wall of the house for them to dry. This was a most tedious and frustrating job for a busy, impatient ten-year-old boy.

The gravel road that wound its way up the valley ended in front of our house. From there, footpaths and a wagon road led further up to the alpine huts and mountains above. Mountaineers from all over Europe would travel to our area to attempt the great climbs accessed from there, sometimes hiring my grandfather to guide them. Often they would ask to store their bicycles or motorcycles in our woodshed.

Many of the famous climbers of the time passed through my domain, and I knew them all. There was Ertl, Frauenberger, Aschenbrenner, Dulfer, Hinterstoiser and Kurz, the Schmidt Brothers, Hechmair and many others. Some of them are still there now, in the little graveyard behind the church. I would watch and listen to these men in awe, always impressed by what a friendly, happy lot they were. While they climbed, I guarded their belongings with my life.

One day, one of these fellows gave me a piton. I couldn't believe my luck — a genuine, slightly used, rusty rock piton. In my mind, pitons were synonymous with rappelling, so with gift in hand, I rushed immediately to the work shed to get a hammer and an old piece of rope. Then I climbed up on the house roof and drove the piton into the chimney. I tied one end of the rope to the piton and the other I threw over the edge of the roof. The bottom end of it was at least four metres from the ground, but that didn't slow my enthusiasm. I placed the rope between my legs, up across my chest and over my shoulder just like Dulfer had shown me. Feet apart, I leaned back ready to begin my descent when... the piton came out! Down I went, rapidly gaining speed as I schussed down the shingled roof, flat on my back and head first. Remember, the house was three stories high. There was a set of telephone wires at the second-floor level with which I made my first contact. The wires tossed me against the wall of the house. Down the wall I went… straight into Grandmother's flowers. I tried to grab hold of the centre tray of flowers as my legs hit and broke the bottom tray, but the brackets holding both came out of the wall and I continued on down.

Flowers, trays, dirt, brackets and I, with the rope still wrapped around me, were all falling as one — and then the real disaster happened! I landed on Grandfather's shingles and the entire pile fell over. It took me weeks to straighten those damn things out.

What I considered the biggest stroke of luck though, was that when I was on the ground, flat out among the flowers and shingles and dirt, one of the flowerpots, in delayed action, fell out of its hanger and hit me on the head, knocking me unconscious. This prevented me from getting the biggest spanking of my life.

Thinking of it now, I have that flowerpot to thank for me spending my life in the business of mountaineering.

Injuries aside, that experience left me eager to climb my first real mountain. Every chance I had, I pestered my grandfather to take me climbing with him. The following summer, I saw my opportunity. My Aunt Liesl came from Salzburg with some of her friends for a visit. While there, they wanted to climb Hochkonig, the 2,941-metre peak directly behind our house, with Grandfather.

At the time, like most of the kids in our village, I had only one pair of large-sized boots, which were meant to last me for years. I would begin wearing the boots in the fall when the snow fell and would store them away in the spring when most of the snow had melted. Throughout the summer, I went barefoot.

Our family
home minus
the flowers.

Aunt Liesl didn't have any boots appropriate for climbing, and without thinking to consult me she asked Grandfather if she could use mine. He agreed. They knew I wanted to climb the mountain and wouldn't want to lend her my boots, so in order to get me out of their hair they sent me on an errand just before they left for their climb.

Grandfather had done some carpentry work on a place called Berka Haus, a two-hour walk from our home, and the family there still owed him some money. They sent me there to collect the money. Although they tried to keep it from me, I already knew of their plans. I ran all the way to Berka Haus, barefoot as usual, got the money and ran back home. When I returned, they were gone. I knew they were headed up to the alpine hut at the base of the route that day and planned to begin the climb the next morning.

I also knew that near the top of the mountain, climbers had to cross a glacier before continuing up to the summit. My feet were so toughened up from being barefoot all the time that I knew I could handle the lower part of the mountain without boots, but not the glacier. Pig-headed and absolutely determined to join them, I went from house to house in our village to borrow a pair. Not surprisingly, no one wanted to lend me any. Finally, I arrived at the door of one guy who made his own boots. Those boots had a leather upper portion nailed to a carved wooden sole. Reluctantly he agreed to let me use them, so off I went.

Just before Grandfather, Aunt Liesl and her friends bedded down for the night, I arrived at the alpine hut. The borrowed pair of boots were tied together and hung around my neck. Due to the stiffness of the solid wood sole, it was difficult to walk in them. I was far more comfortable in bare feet.

Nothing Aunt Liesl or Grandfather said convinced me to return home; in the end, they were forced to take me with them. The next day, I carried the boots all the way up to the snowline. Then I put them on and walked across the glacier. The snow on the glacier gave way under my feet, so it was possible to walk that section in the stiff boots. Once we travelled across the glacier, I took them off again. Standing on top of a mountain for the first time was a great feeling, but I think even then it was the actual process of climbing and descending that held my interest more than standing on the summit.

When we arrived home that evening, I had supper and went down to the woodpile to play with the other kids. I gave the guy his boots back. They didn't have a scratch on them, because I had only used them to cross the glacier. That was my first mountain.

As a kid, I grew up with my grandparents. I never met my father, and my mother had married another guy. At one point, when I was about eleven, she decided she wanted me back, and I was sent to live with her, my stepfather and my seven half-brothers and sisters. I hated my new home for many reasons, one of which was that I was gone from the mountains. So after a few weeks, I ran away. I walked all the way back to Muhlbach, a distance of about two hundred kilometres, which took me about two weeks, sleeping in ditches at night and finding food where I could. After that, I never left the mountains again.

Grandfather was real a mountain man and he liked my drive for the mountains. Once when I was a teenager, I went to a climbing course in a different part of Austria. At the time, everybody, including my grandfather, simply tied their climbing ropes around their waists. At the climbing school, I was taught that this was not safe. If you fell, the jerk on the rope could break your back, or you could end up hanging upside down. They showed us how to tie it around our chests instead. My grandfather had already spent more than forty years in the business of mountaineering, but like a typical teenager, I came home and immediately told him that his way of tying-in was for the birds.

Grandfather had a bushy moustache and when he got angry that moustache would start to twitch. Well, the thing started to twitch. He was a tall man and I knew all about his temper, so I started to back off. Finally, he spoke. "Well, we'll go down to the practice cliff and you show me," he said.

Off we went and I tied him in the way I'd been taught. Then we just let ourselves hang there on the side of the cliff. We didn't try to fall onto the rope or anything like that. He was hanging there and I was hanging there, just trying it out. He didn't say anything the whole time or on the way home either. A little while later, though, he finally spoke. "Yup, you're right. Your way is better. I'll change."

I thought he was ten feet tall when he said that. Here was a guy with forty years experience and a teenager telling him that he was doing things wrong. But he listened and he changed. That was an attitude I tried to keep all my life. Every time something new came around, I would try it. If it was good I adopted it, and if it was junk or a fad, I let it go.

When I was about twenty, I began competing in Nordic Combined, a very popular sport in Europe at the time. The best ski jumping scores combined with the fastest cross-country ski racing times produced a winner. I succeeded to where I was ranked fourth in Austria. My much older teammate but good friend, Sepp Bradl, was world champion.

Most of the competitions I took part in went well and I had some great results, but sometimes things went terribly wrong. One year, for example, the Austrian Championships were held at Bishofshoven, a larger town not far from Muhlbach, well known for its world-class ski jump.

Unfortunately, on the afternoon that the ski jumping portion of the competition was scheduled to take place, a gusty wind was blowing. This was potentially dangerous for ski jumpers in mid-flight. However, numerous preparations had been made to organize the event and a large crowd had shown up to watch, so the officials let the competition run. I was the eighth competitor scheduled to jump. The first seven all managed reasonable jumps, without problems from the wind.

Rather than give each competitor a short time limit in which to start his jump, due to the wind situation, event officials decided to leave it up to the jumpers to choose when to go. When it was my turn, the wind picked up. So there I was, sitting on the narrow bench at the top of the jump, waiting for it to die down. I was watching a small flag a short distance away in order to determine the strength and direction of the wind. I delayed the jump for several minutes, but the wind just kept blowing. It became obvious that the large crowd below was getting impatient. Finally the flag sagged a bit and I signaled to the officials that I was ready to jump.

I sped down the ramp with no problems, but when I took off a sudden gust of wind caught my skis and blew them back behind me. I was flying through the air spread-eagle, with the backs of my skis almost touching the back of my head. Below me, I could hear a loud gasp from the crowd. Somehow in the air I managed to get my skis underneath me, but after flying about seventy metres, I landed with my skis sideways to the hill and piled up something terrible.

As a result of the fall, I must have suffered a concussion, but in those days no one bothered to check you out. They saw me get up and walk away from the hill, so they assumed I was okay.

The officials did however decide to postpone the competition after my fall.

One of the people in the audience that day was a famous Austrian film starlet named Maria Schell. Shortly after the competition was called off, they lined up the Austrian team to be introduced to her. Since she was a beautiful woman, this was no hardship for any of us. She started at one end of the line, shaking each guy's hand and saying a few words.

When she got to me, I looked at her and reached out to shake her hand. I remember thinking, I can see her lips moving but why isn't she saying anything? She started getting smaller and smaller and further away from me. Then suddenly everything went black and I fell to the ground. Talk about embarrassing! It was due to the concussion of course, but that didn't stop the guys from razzing me forever. They made it out that I was so taken by that beautiful woman that I collapsed at her feet.

While still in Austria, I honed my climbing skills on many of the more difficult routes in the Alps.

Just before I left Austria for Canada, I helped with two rescues that left a permanent impression on me. One of these was on the mountain Dachstein. In those days we didn't have walkie-talkies or any other type of verbal communication system, so we used mirrors to blink signals at each other.

I was rappelling down to the accident site when the rescuers on the ridge above me blinked a signal. I didn't know what was going on, so I stopped and they pulled me back up. When I reached the ridge, they told me that the two rescuers who had rappelled down just before me had fallen off and had been killed. I don't know exactly what happened, but I think one fell and pulled the other off. I clearly remember that incident to this day. In the end, we managed to complete the rescue, but at the cost of two rescuers. Years later, when I was in charge of rescues, I always tried to keep things as safe as possible for the rescue team. It was no use creating a bigger accident than we already had.

The second accident involved ten kids and three teachers caught in a snowstorm. They were visiting from a flatland area of Germany and while in the mountains, decided to hike up to a high plateau. When they reached the plateau, it began to snow heavily and they had trouble getting down. It was decided that the group would stay in one place while one teacher and a couple of the kids would go for help. They didn't make it.

I was part of the search party sent out to go and look for the group when they didn't return that night. All thirteen of them perished. I feel this accident could have been entirely prevented if they had taken along someone with knowledge of the mountains, ideally a guide. During my years in the rescue business, we had a number of incidents that involved youth groups, some with tragic consequences. These accidents were always particularly distressing to me.

The two rescues in Austria taught me very profound and lasting lessons. Looking back, they foreshadowed some of the main things that I worked hard to prevent in Canada.

Mount
Sir Donald in
winter.

2

THE SIDEHILLGOUGER SAYS,

"There are only two ways to become famous as
a mountaineer – have an accident or write a book.
I recommend the second option."

IN LATE 1955, I travelled to Canada with friend and fellow mountaineer, Frank Stark. We worked at a Laurentian ski resort for the winter and then decided to drive west to see the famous Rocky Mountains.

We drove across the country in Frank's old Dodge, all of our worldly belongings stuffed in the back, taking odd jobs along the way to pay for food and gas. Near the end of the trip, we completely ran out of money and had to wire friends who were already out west, to borrow some.

After many days of travelling, the mountains came into view just west of Calgary. Frank stopped the car on the side of the road and we jumped out. Seeing the Rockies for the first time was overwhelming for both of us. Neither of us knew then that we would spend the rest of our lives in their shadow.

The five years that followed that single moment were a time of learning, discovery and firsts for me. It all started later that summer, when I landed my first and only job as a horse wrangler.

I was hired by legendary outfitter Bill Harrison, who had lined up two groups of clients to explore the Rogers Pass area on horseback. If I remember correctly, the first group was the Iowa Mountaineering Club and the second was the Genesee Valley Hiking Club. Each trip would be two weeks.

At the time, there was no road to Rogers Pass, so we shipped eighteen head of horses, the gear and ourselves in by rail, and set up camp in the Asulkan Valley. I helped Bill with the horse wrangling and if clients wanted a guide, I took them hiking and scrambling in the mountains.

From our camp, I could see Mount Sir Donald, a beautiful pointed peak rising up to a height of 3,277 metres. It looked like a challenging climb and I was immediately interested in making it my first in Canada. I asked Bill if I could go and he agreed *if* I finished my work first.

On the day of my planned climb, I woke at four in the morning and went to catch the horses, which had wandered a number of kilometres further up the Asulkan Valley during the night. When I returned, Bill and I saddled them and then made breakfast for the guests. After that I set off at a run to the base of the mountain. I climbed the northeast ridge, solo without a rope, reaching the top just after the noon hour. (I actually wasn't wearing a watch, but Bill and the guests watched the entire climb from below and told me that later.) I managed to make it back down to camp in time for a late supper. It was a really enjoyable climb.

You didn't know they had cowboys in Austria.

Meanwhile that day, two horses had lost shoes and Bill had re-shod them. After supper, he asked me to take those horses at least part way up the trail towards the pasture, so they could join the other horses. I put a bridle on one of them and rode him bareback. I knew the horse I was riding spooked easily, but there wasn't much I could do to ease his fear. We were moving along the trail quite fast, because these two horses wanted to join the others up in the pasture and I just wanted to return to camp and relax.

We came around a corner and all of a sudden there was a tree across the trail. Without hesitation, the horse I was on jumped up on the bank at the side of the trail to avoid the windfall. I was swiped off, and the horse, free of my weight, immediately took off up the trail, its reins hanging down in front. I knew I couldn't leave the horse overnight with the reins hanging down like that, so I was forced to run the remaining few kilometres up to the pasture to where the horses were grazing, to remove those reins. That shit horse was hard to catch, but I finally got the bridle off and headed back to camp. That was one long day.

After the trip, when all the guests had left on the train, Bill decided that we should ride back to his home, rather than loading all the horses on the train again. So Bill, his three children and one of their friends (all of whom were in their early teens), eighteen head of horses and I rode back up over Rogers Pass, down to Bear Creek, up the rivers Beaver, Grizzly and Copperstain, and along the ridge to Duncan Pass. We couldn't access the mountains south of there with the horses, so we backtracked a bit. We went up and over Bald Mountain and then followed the Spillamacheen River all the way down to the Columbia. After crossing the Columbia River, we headed up the western slopes of the Rockies until we reached Bill's hunting ground near Kootenay Crossing. The ride was more than 320 kilometres and took slightly longer than two weeks.

One beautiful, blue-sky day up near Duncan Pass, I was riding at the back of the pack enjoying the fall colours in the ground vegetation that surrounded us. In the distance, I saw my first grizzly bear. A short time later, I watched the unsaddled horses cross a creek and then charge up onto a ridge in front of me, the wind blowing through their manes and tails. Behind them the Great Glacier hung down between the towering Rogers Pass Selkirks. The whole scene took my breath away. Up until then, I had assumed I would eventually head back to Austria to live, but there on that skyline, at that moment, looking at those horses and the mountains behind, I decided Canada was the place for me. This was where I would stay.

During that next winter I skied a lot in Banff and Kimberly, and befriended a guy by the name of Sam Warmington. He owned a ski shop in Kimberly. We talked about what type of work I should pursue and what I would most like to do. I admitted that I would like to have a ski shop like his and he replied, "Yah that's a good idea. Why don't you?"

We discussed several good options in regards to where I should open a shop. The Lake Louise Ski Area was in operation and it needed a ski instructor, as well as a ski shop. Blairmore, in the Crowsnest Pass, was another place to consider. Finally, there was Vernon or Jasper. I had driven to the Columbia Icefields area of Jasper National Park once in the summer and had looked around a little bit. I was impressed with the mountains there and so in the end, I decided on Jasper.

That fall, I packed up my old station wagon and headed to Jasper to open a ski shop. Sam gave me some equipment to sell in my store. En route, I stopped at Monods in Banff and

John Monod, the owner, also gave me a few items to get me started.

In my pocket, I carried a letter of recommendation from Sam to the president of the ski club in Jasper. When I arrived there, I drove down the main street to check it out and saw a woman pushing a baby buggy. Behind her was a little girl crying. I could see that her shoelaces were untied, so I stopped and jumped out of my car to tie the little girl's laces. Then I asked the woman if she happened to know the president of the local ski club. "Yes," she said, "that's my husband."

So off we went to her house where I met her husband, Aubrey Anderson. I showed him the letter of recommendation from Sam and he said, "Well, we have this porch out front here that you can use for your shop if you clean it out. You can live in the room downstairs if you want to, but we are going on holiday tomorrow morning, so you will just have to look after yourself."

After knowing them for about an hour, I moved into the Anderson's home and they promptly left on their two-week vacation. There I was, on my own in Jasper, ready to start up my first business.

As a businessman, I felt I had everything going for me: I didn't know anybody in town; I didn't have any money; I could hardly speak English; and I had never run a business before. I was going to make it for sure.

As unlikely as it seemed, I managed to get everything set up and open for business, but at the start sales were very slow. When the first snow came though, people saw me ski and after that everything changed. All of a sudden, there were people in the store and things started to hustle. The biggest problem was

providing good stock to sell. It was difficult to find a supplier, even in Calgary. There was not a pair of skis available anywhere that I considered usable. The equipment that I could buy was outdated and of poor quality. To better my business the following year, I ordered a shipment through a friend in Austria, but that stuff was not great either. My shop did okay, but it would have done much better if I had decent equipment to sell.

At that time, in the late 1950s, we used double-laced leather boots that were lower than mid-shin height. For the most part, the skis we had were wood, although Head Ski Corporation had come out with metal skis a year or two earlier. The bindings were either cable or what we called *long lanyards (or long thongs)*, which were basically long leather straps attached to little rings on the sides of your skis near the boots. The skis had a toe piece, which you placed your boot into. Then you simply wrapped the straps around your boots as tightly as you could to hold the skis to your feet.

In Jasper, I started coaching the Alberta Ski Team. We trained mainly at Jasper's first small ski area on Whistlers Mountain. During the time I was coach, the kids, boys and girls, won twelve Canadian Championships and four scholarships. Ski competitions were divided into four categories: cross country, jumping, slalom and downhill. To win the combined award, a skier had to be good in all four disciplines.

Besides skiing on the hill in the winter, the team and I found plenty of other things to do. We explored Maligne Canyon and climbed ice falls in there. That was before ice tools and ice screws had even been invented. We ski toured a lot, with Watchtower and Shangri-La cabins, and the Tonquin Valley being some of our favourite destinations.

In the summers, I climbed a great deal, sometimes with old friends visiting from Europe and sometimes with new friends from Canada. One Saturday, Artie Kiegl and I put in a difficult new route to Ashlar ridge, after carefully studying the rock face from down below. Ashlar Ridge can be seen to the left as you drive up to Miette Hot Springs. Near the top of the climb was a very difficult slab with no handholds. At the start of this slab was a gulley that came to a point formed by two small ledges about five centimetres wide, one veering up to the right, the other to the left.

On that first ascent, I arrived at the gulley part of the slab and was standing there awkwardly with one foot on one ledge with my toe pointing down to the right, and my other foot on the other ledge pointing up to the right. I was hooked into a piton right in front of me. Artie was a rope length below. At that moment a thunderstorm hit. It was really scary because we were completely exposed there. Then it began to rain. The rainwater poured down that gulley and jumped straight out at me. I was so soaked that I had to pull my knickers open at the knees to let all of the water out of my pants. We both stood there on that face for a long while until the weather finally cleared. We still had the most difficult part of the route to climb.

On Roche Pertrix, we put in a new route on the left side of the west face, which I believe was more difficult than Ashlar Ridge. On one section you had to traverse a full rope length, hook on a piton, traverse back, and then swing over.

Some of the other more difficult climbs included the south face of Colin, which I did with Ramsey Heckley. We put a new route right up the middle of the face. We also put routes up the

Well suited up for the climb —
bandana, modern climbing pants
and rock shoes — thirty years
ahead of our time!

two easterly summits of the Queen Elizabeth Range of mountains, and two new routes up the Medicine Slabs.

One summer, we spent a number of weeks up at Maligne Lake and climbed almost every mountain in the area. At the Columbia Icefields we climbed the Skyladder of Andromeda and the north face of Athabasca. I don't know if those routes had been climbed before us or not. I spent quite a bit of time in Banff, and at the Bugaboos, too.

During those first few years in Canada, people continuously asked me why I climbed mountains. This question baffled me. In Austria, we never asked *why*. It was just part of what we did, part of our culture. Why didn't people question other activities? Why, for example, was it totally acceptable for someone to put on a pair of shorts and jogging shoes and then run around in a circle? The guy would end up in exactly the same spot he started from, and then he would do it again. And nobody seemed to question that.

I often climbed with Tony Messner, a very well-known German climber. He had completed many difficult climbs in Europe, like the Gran Sasso and the north face of the Eiger. Later, Tony would be an examiner on my mountain guide's exam.

One time, Tony and I decided to try the first winter ascent on the north face of Mount Robson, the highest and, arguably, the most difficult peak in the Canadian Rockies to climb. At 3,954 metres, it has a 3,129-metre rise from the base. We were about fifteen years ahead of our time. We had made it well over halfway up when the temperature plummeted to thirty below. We had never encountered those types of temperatures in Europe and were not prepared, so we pulled back and luckily didn't freeze anything. I am fairly sure though that if the weather had held, we would have made it.

In the summers, I also started mountain guiding. Generally, I earned $25.00 a day for guiding a client up a mountain. An attempt on Mount Robson, which was a much more difficult mountain and took at least two days to climb, earned me $100.00. Mount Edith Cavell, a beautiful mountain within view of the town site of Jasper, was my bread and butter in those days. I climbed it almost once a week with clients in the summer at $30.00 a day.

Every so often when I was guiding, someone would arrive and want to climb a mountain that had never been climbed before. These folks thought that here in the backwoods of Canada in the 1950s, unclimbed mountains were still readily available. Of course they also preferred a mountain that was not too difficult to climb and didn't have a long approach route.

Well, I knew of one such mountain. It was a pointy peak in the Colin Range across the river from Jasper and it paid well. A first-ascent mountain earned me $20.00 on top of my regular fee.

It all started one day when a tall, older man with a big belly walked into my store. He introduced himself as Mr. P. from Cape Town, South Africa.

He said, "You have been recommended as the best mountain guide in Jasper."

I answered, "Yah, well, I am the only one."

He said, "I have heard there are many unclimbed mountains in the Rockies. I would like to engage you for one of these first accents. As you can see, I am not a young man anymore, so the climb should not be too strenuous."

Now, it so happened that a few days earlier, Tony Messner and I had gone into the Colin Range to put a new route up the NW ridge of Colin 2, now known as Messner Ridge. On that first attempt, the weather was not good enough for such a difficult climb, so we decided to climb a pointed peak with the smooth slab to the left of where we were. We reached the summit without any difficulty, built a little cairn, smoked our pipes and returned home.

When Mr. P. hired me, I thought this would be a great climb for him. I said something to the effect of, "Across the valley… pointed peak… slab on the left… not sure it has been climbed yet… let's find out anyway." Off we went the next day, up the south slab. Near the top, I had him stop a full rope length below the summit. I climbed to the peak, knocked the cairn down the north side of the mountain, levelled everything off and then hauled him up. I congratulated him for the first ascent and we built a cairn to mark his success. I asked him what his wife's name was and he said Hildegard and I said, "Okay, we'll call this mountain Mount Hildegard." I had a small blank book with me for use as a summit log. We wrote a little blurb about the climb, signed our names and inserted the book into the cairn. Then I lowered him down the first rope length. I levelled everything off, pocketed the summit log and headed down the mountain with Mr. P.

Well, it didn't take very long before I got another call. There was this guy staying at Jasper Park Lodge. He had a great big belly, but said he was an experienced mountaineer. He wanted to climb Mount Edith Cavell or Mount Robson or something like that. I looked at his belly and thought, "well, you are a mountaineer all right — you've brought along your own overhang." But he was quite adamant. He had after all, climbed the Matterhorn — twenty years ago. So I told him about the pointy peak across the valley. I said, "Well, I know of one mountain there in the Colin Range and I am quite sure it would be a first ascent. Let's find out anyway."

So off we went. At the summit I congratulated him. "What's your wife's name?" I asked. Gertrude. "Okay, I hereby name this mountain Mount Gertrude." We built a cairn, started a new book and took pictures. Then he headed down, I grabbed the book, pushed the cairn down the north side and followed him.

A few weeks later, there came another one. We made it to the summit and I congratulated him and we named the mountain after his wife.

Now, Tony Messner had a habit of chewing prune stones. He must have been chewing one earlier in the summer when we climbed the mountain, because suddenly this guy notices a prune stone lying between the rocks. He picks it up, looks at me quite annoyed and says, "Somebody has been up here already. This isn't a first ascent!"

I immediately said, "No, no, that's my prune stone."

I took it from him, popped it into my mouth and started to chew. Then down we went.

After a while, a lot of people, including the Alpine Club of Canada, caught wind of what I was doing and they unofficially named the peak First Ascent Mountain. I think the mountain naming committee in Ottawa has officially dubbed it Lectern Peak, but to me it will always be First Ascent Mountain.

In the winter following those climbs, I had my first really close call in the mountains. Four of us, including my friend Googs (Gabrielle Koebel née Morin), Tony Messner and another guy, undertook a winter ascent on Mount Edith Cavell. We walked un-roped up the west side to the summit buttress. Soon after, we arrived at the ridge that we needed to cross in order to reach the summit cairn.

The summit ridge on Mount Edith Cavell is about half to one metre wide for most of the distance across. On our right, the north face of the mountain fell 1,524 metres almost straight down to the small glacial lake below. Wind blew up the south side of the mountain and when it hit the colder air coming up from the north, over time it formed a cornice on the north side of the ridge.

Tony and the other guy were ahead of us. It was snowing and blowing a bit and Googs and I just wandered along slowly, making our way across. The two in front had walked across a cornice without noticing it, and without paying much attention, I followed their footprints in the snow. Suddenly I heard a sound like a rifle shot. I thought to myself, "Oh, a cornice broke off some-place." Then I felt something move. I looked down and saw a crack open up between my legs. It threw me off balance immediately. The only thing I could do was jump straight up. I fell into the fast-widening crack, turning in mid air and landing on my fore-arms. My elbows and upper part of my body were hanging over the 1,500-metre north face. I was looking straight up into the sky and could hear the chunk of ice that had just broken off splinter into a million pieces on its way down the mountain. The entire thing happened so fast.

Seconds before the ice cracked, I had looked over my left shoulder and could see Googs walking along behind me. After the cornice broke, I looked over my shoulder again. No Googs. This really scared me. I thought she had gone down with the cornice.

Then I looked to my right and there she was, out of harm's way. I hadn't taken into account that I had turned during the fall.

Had things been different, I could have fallen more than 1,500 metres down the north face of Cavell. I hope that those of you reading this now will learn as much from it as I did that day.

In those early years, I gained several skills that helped me a great deal as time went by. The first of these was that I learned how to read people. If a client came in and had never climbed a mountain before, I needed to quickly figure out how difficult and high a mountain that person could successfully climb while still posing a challenge. A person's level of fitness was usually fairly easy to determine, but I also had to assess his or her perseverance, level of fear and ability to trust me as the guide. I was, after all, responsible for getting people safely up and down a mountain. If people listened to me and did what I said, I could get first-time climbers up and down some fairly difficult mountains; however, if they wanted to tell me how to do my job and I could expect them to do something sudden and unsafe, we wouldn't get very far. I found that men who were used to being in charge found it difficult to release control. Also, a man with a bruised ego could be a very dangerous thing. At times, I had to use some creative tactics to keep people safe.

One summer in the late 1950s, I guided a regular client, Dr. M. and his inexperienced friend. Dr. M. was a well-known professor from New York City who hired me for the first two weeks in August annually for six years. He said to me once, "I come to you because of your philosophy."

Curious, I said, "What philosophy do I have? I'm not the one who has studied the great philosophers."

"Nevertheless," he said, "I come here because of your philosophy."

Every year he brought somebody with him. One year his wife came, and being kind of a sly guy, he would always have her carry a heavier load than he did. He talked her into it and she seemed totally satisfied that this was the way things should be.

Another year, he brought a football hero. Well over six feet tall, with big shoulders and narrow hips, he was a good-looking guy, but loud. We went off to the Fryatt Valley for a few days to climb some of the mountains there. Hans Schwarz, a mountaineer who later took over my guiding business, and I had built a tent-frame as a place to stay when we visited that beautiful valley.

With Dr. M. in Fryatt Valley.

Years later we helped build a hut in the same spot, which still stands today. My two clients and I had a lot of gear, so I brought along my horse, Bubbles, to help pack some of the stuff.

The first day, the three of us decided to climb Karpathos Peak. The football-player guy was third on the rope. We climbed about halfway up when the doctor told me that his friend was finished. He wanted to go back to camp and wasn't interested in climbing any further. The doctor of course wanted to continue, but we couldn't just leave the guy there or send him down alone. Instead we decided to push him to continue. Using several tactics we finally managed to cajole him up to the top. By then, the guy wasn't interested in anything or anybody. He didn't look around. He didn't take any pictures.

After lunch and a rest, we went off the back of the mountain and down. When we reached the meadow, the young guy kept looking back up at the mountain and began to smile. He was satisfied that he had climbed it.

The doctor wanted to climb another mountain named Xerxes the next day, but I knew his friend would not care to join us. So here I would have a guy with a bit of a bruised ego sitting around the tent all day. What was he going to do? He needed to feel like a man and I knew that he would probably do something stupid to prove it. There was a big waterfall down below us, a cave system and waterfalls above, and of course, several mountains and cliffs all around — numerous places where a guy could get into trouble if left alone all day. I had to think of something to keep him safe while the doctor and I climbed Xerxes Peak.

We sat around for a while in the evening after our climb up Mount Karpathos and I finally said to the doctor, "After we climb Xerxes tomorrow, maybe the next day we can climb the little peak behind us, over in the middle of the meadow. It is a real nice mountain. It's pointy so a little bit of climbing has to be done, but it would be really nice. It might even be a first ascent."

The doctor asked, "Why haven't you climbed it yet?"

I said, "I just didn't have the right climbing partner and you know, I just never got around to it. It would be really nice though, because you could sleep a little longer. Eight o'clock would be a good time to start out. We'd just have to pass the out-house and then up the trail behind it. That trail leads through the bush, up to the alp lands and then to the base of this little mountain. It would be a real nice climb, an easier one, but with some difficult stretches. I think the day after tomorrow we will give it a try."

The next day the doctor and I took off early in the morning to climb Xerxes. Just before eight o'clock in the morning, I stopped and we took a short rest. We had a clear view of the tent down below.

I said to the doctor, "Now watch this. Your friend is going to come out of the tent at eight, and he's going to have his ruck-sack packed and his funny hat. He will walk past the outhouse, follow that trail up behind it and go climb that little mountain back there. I told you about it yesterday. Remember?"

The doctor had only half listened to me the night before. Sure enough, at just a few minutes past eight, the football hero stepped out of the tent, all dressed and ready to go, with his rucksack on his back, an ice axe and his funny hat. As he started off, he looked up and waved to us.

The doctor asked, "How did you know all this?"

I said, "Well, I kind of told him last night. When I was telling you about the little mountain, I made sure to describe what to do and how to go about doing it. I had to give him something to do today, otherwise he was going to make us trouble. He could have climbed around the waterfall and fallen down or something like that."

So the guy did exactly what I had talked about. He climbed that little peak and returned to the tent before us. We could see him down below as we came off the mountain. He was cooking and singing and whistling — in a really good mood. Just as we reached a little hump across the creek from the tent, we saw him drain a big pot of spaghetti and put it on a little bench. He forgot to put the lid back on the pot. Well, my horse, Bubbles, was standing there and when he turned his back, the horse put his head into the pot. When Bubbles lifted his head back out, noodles were hanging down like whiskers from his nose. That horse slung the whole pot of spaghetti down in one gulp. That's the story of the mountain philosopher.

The second thing I learned during that time was to trust my gut feelings. Of course gut feelings are no replacement for good planning, preparation and knowledge, but sometimes when I had done all of those things and everything seemed fine, my body would let me know otherwise. The first time this happened, I chose not to listen.

I was guiding four students who had just graduated from the University of Alberta. They had decided that as a graduation gift to themselves they would go on a ski touring trip in the mountains. We went to Shangri-La, a beautiful valley with a small cabin, this one in the Maligne Range. The day after our arrival at the cabin, we decided to climb Mount Aberhart, a smaller rounded mountain, on skis.

With skins attached to the bottom of our skis (to prevent us from sliding back), we climbed about two-thirds of the way up on the north side when we came to an avalanche slope. I wanted to cross to the other side in order to continue on our way up the mountain, so I told the students to stay behind in a safe spot and I would go first. I prepared myself by taking my hands out of the straps of the ski poles, slinging my rucksack over one shoulder and getting my skis ready to eject. There were three snow-covered grassy humps spaced out across the slope and I moved from one to the other. After the second hump, I moved a little further onto the slope. All of a sudden my body wouldn't function any more. I can't say why or what happened, but my legs just would not move forward. I couldn't safely make a kick turn on that slope, so I backed off, which was a little difficult with skins on my skis. I reached the first hump then was able to turn around and ski back to the students.

I said, "This is not going to work. We have to go someplace else." I found another way up to the top and we had a great time skiing down.

At lunch one guy asked, "What happened up there?"

I said, "I don't know. I really don't know, but if you like, we can go back up and look at it again. Maybe we can find out why that happened to me."

Two of the guys decided to stay at the lunch spot, while the other two and I put our skis on and headed back up. When we reached the same spot, I again told the two students to stay behind in a safe place. I stepped onto the avalanche slope the same distance as I had before. At exactly the same spot, the same thing happened again. My body just would not function. I couldn't move any further forward.

Suddenly I felt really angry. What was going on? I stomped my foot in frustration and — the entire mountainside let loose! Down I went. I knew the best reaction if caught in an avalanche was to try to sit back and work with my arms to get the snow in behind me. If I fell forward, the snow would run over my feet and I would be buried in a couple of seconds, but if I could ride it out by sitting down and the snow filled in behind me, I might stand a chance. So that's what I tried to do. Then all I could think was that I couldn't get any air. I was sucking as hard as I could to no avail. There must have been snow particles down in my lungs.

I woke up a little while later with the two guys who had stayed at the lunch spot looking over me. I had ended up pretty well on top of the snow. The two guys had dug me the rest of the way out. We looked around for my equipment but I never found one of my skis until the next summer.

After that, I really trusted that gut feeling and it saved my life several times. Years later, whenever I went on a trip with the wardens and we had to cross a questionable avalanche slope, I never let anyone else cross the slope first. I always crossed it myself, because I knew I could rely on that gut feeling.

The third thing I learned in those early years was the value of humour in guiding, and later on, in training the wardens and performing rescues. A good joke came in handy in many situations. Often for example, new clients would be a bit nervous about their ability to climb a mountain and scared of the dangers. I would stand at the bottom with them, looking up and say something like,

"The first thing you should know about mountaineering is that it's fifty percent uphill." They would laugh and relax.

Years later I told anxious new warden recruits, "If you want to know how to qualify for a job in mountain rescue, put a flashlight to your ear. If light shines out the other side, you're hired."

At the start of a warden school, I would say something like, "Are you ready to quit sucking coffee and spend a little time on the side hill?" It always got them out the door faster.

When I wanted to slow down the keeners at the beginning of a trip, I would say, "You rush on ahead. I'll wait for you on the top," which usually managed to do the trick.

During rescues or on difficult trips, I had to keep everybody alert all the time. I couldn't just have them trudge along thinking about something else because that's when the problems would begin. So I made a joke or said something stupid, which managed to wake them up and focus their attention back on the task at hand.

At different times, I also used humour to motivate the group, to help them remember important points, to get them to move faster, to defuse tense situations or to distract them from their fatigue. Of course, it made things more fun, too.

Base camp at
Mount Logan.

3

THE SIDEHILLGOUGER SAYS,

*"The best piece of equipment you can take with you
into the mountains is your brain."*

ONE SPRING DAY IN 1958, a group of us were skiing at Parker's Ridge near the Columbia Icefields. Hans Gmoser, who later founded Canadian Mountain Holidays helicopter skiing operation, was with us and started talking about Mount Logan. He pointed out that Logan, Canada's highest peak, had only been climbed once via the East Ridge, and not by Canadians. He thought we should find a group of guys and try it. I agreed. From that day, it took us almost a year to organize the whole thing.

Hans put a team together and was named leader of the expedition. Besides Hans and me, the team included Ron Smylie, Karl Richer, Don Lyon and Phillippe Delesalle. Although only one of us had been born in Canada, we were considered the first "all-Canadian" team to climb the mountain.

At 5,959 metres elevation, Mount Logan is the second-highest mountain in North America (after McKinley/Denali), and its base circumference makes it the world's largest massif of non-volcanic mountains. Located in the southwestern corner of the Yukon, it is part of the St. Elias Range, a group of mountains known for their severe weather, excessive snowfall and remoteness. Mount Logan itself stands in the middle of the largest non-polar icefield in the world. In May and June, climbers have a short window in which to attempt the summit.

That first ascent of the East Ridge of Mount Logan was made in 1957 by an American team. From the information we had, after

being flown in and dropped off at the base of the mountain, it took them twenty-four days and nine camps to reach the summit. (Nowadays, those numbers would read more like six camps and ten to twelve days of climbing). We didn't have that much time or money.

We were on a shoestring budget. After pooling everything we had, we came up with a grand total of $1,500. A national newspaper promised to give us another $1,500 if we let them publish the story and photographs of the trip upon our return. With flights north, and then into base camp, plus equipment and food, an expedition on Mount Logan these days would cost no less than $25,000.

A word from our sponsor.

Don and Karl
making their way
to Whitehorse.

We bought most of our equipment at an army surplus store in Calgary. There was better equipment available at the time, but we didn't have the money to buy it. Head Ski Corporation provided us with skis, though we had to pay for the bindings. For footwear, we bought Kodiak insulated work boots and army mukluks at $3 a pair. Then we fitted the mukluks onto the skis.

The people of Jasper were very interested in the trip and supported me in many ways. Some of them helped by making willow wands that would be placed for visibility when travelling across the glaciers in potential whiteout conditions. Others organized food.

When we had everything together — ski touring equipment, warm clothing, sleeping bags, tents, food, cooking items and

other necessary supplies — we loaded up my old Plymouth. The car was crammed with gear for the six of us. Smiley and I then drove up to Whitehorse, but we had so little money that the other four had to hitchhike.

Hans had decided to make a film about the trip and began filming the day we left. We drove north on the Alaska Highway, beginning at mile zero at Dawson Creek. In those days, at Fort St. John, fifty miles up the highway, the pavement suddenly ended and the endless winding gravel road began, causing us to wonder if the crew that had built the 'highway' had been paid by the mile. The highway has since been straightened out and paved.

The team in front of our headquarters: from the left Ron, Karl, Hans, Don, Phillippe and yours truly.

A couple of the guys managed to arrive in Whitehorse before Smiley and me. At the time there were a lot of empty old shacks scattered around, homes to the gold miners when they came into town to resupply. However, since the miners were already out at their mine sites, we picked one of those shacks and moved right in. We put a sign up to the left of the door that read *Logan Expedition 1959*, and made that place our headquarters.

In May 1959, Whitehorse was a real shantytown. The rundown shacks were everywhere, and there were no sidewalks, no paved roads, nothing. After spending a few days there preparing for our trip, we left to climb the mountain. Four weeks later, when we returned to Whitehorse, we were shocked to see that all of the old shacks were gone, numerous roads had been paved and there were sidewalks down the main street. The city had taken a Caterpillar to it all and pushed everything down. The reason: the Queen of England was scheduled to visit in July.

While in Whitehorse, we hired a fixed-wing plane to airdrop a supply of food at East Logan Glacier near the base of the mountain, and to drop another load at the base of the Donjek Glacier with rubber dinghies for the trip out. We didn't have the money to be airlifted in ourselves, so we skied two hundred kilometres, mostly on glaciers, to the base of the mountain.

Starting off on May 28, 1959, we walked up the Slims River until we reached the base of the Kaskawulsh Glacier. On skis, we travelled up the one-hundred-plus-kilometre-long Kaskawulsh Glacier, down the Hubbard Glacier and finally onto the East Logan Glacier. It was the first, and I believe only time skis were used to get to the mountain. To this date, the trip has never been repeated. It's simply too far.

Our route.

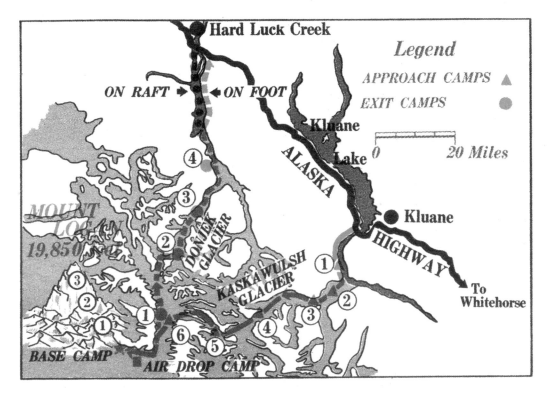

Hard Luck Creek

Legend

APPROACH CAMPS ▲

EXIT CAMPS ●

ON RAFT → ← ON FOOT

Kluane Lake

ALASKA

0   20 Miles

④

③

MOUNT
LOGAN
19,850

②

DONJEK
GLACIER

Kluane

HIGHWAY

③

①

KASKAWULSH
GLACIER

①

To
Whitehorse

②

②

①

③

④

BASE CAMP

⑥   ⑤

AIR DROP CAMP

In our thirty-five-kilogram packs, we carried all our gear and food supplies for ten days, unable to predict how quickly we would be able to cover the two hundred kilometres of primarily glacier travel. We skied about thirty to forty-five kilometres daily, so by the evening of the fifth day, it looked as if we would make it to our airdrop by the following afternoon. However, there were high cirrus clouds developing overhead and I started to worry about snow. If it snowed that night and covered up our airdrop, then we might have trouble finding it. The food we were carrying was not enough to complete the trip, so without the airdrop supplies, we would be forced to turn around and go home.

We had travelled all day long, but Hans and I decided to continue in order to reach the East Logan Glacier and our destined airdrop before it was buried. We left instructions with our teammates, packed up and travelled all night (another forty-five kilometres) to the possibly hidden cache. Thankfully, it was early June in the north, so it was light most of the night.

In the meantime, the other guys made camp. Hans and I arrived at our destination the next morning and started looking for the stuff dropped from the plane. It had snowed a bit during the night, but not as much as we feared. Our supplies were spread over quite a distance, but we found everything except for one package that contained all the noodles. That one must have fallen down a crevasse.

We set up our tent and at ten o'clock in the morning, crawled into our sleeping bags, half dead, and slept. Later in the afternoon, our friends arrived.

On the ridge of Mount Logan at 4,420 metres.
Camp 1 and the knife ridge at 3,658 metres
are below. Notice the Trapper Nelson packs
and the mukluks. We weren't hindered
by modern equipment.

Finally we were at the base of the mountain. Base camp was at an altitude of 2,377 metres above sea level, so ahead of us stood a 3,658-metre rise to the peak. As stated earlier, in modern expeditions, climbers generally make six high camps and take between ten and twelve days to reach the summit.

We had three high camps, the first at an altitude of 3,291 metres, the second at 4,389 metres, and the third at 5,182 metres. On June 12, 1959, six days after we left base camp, we reached the summit — all six of us. Six days in, six days to the summit, one day all the way down, and ten days out — twenty-three days round-trip.

Here we are at 5,334 metres —
625 vertical metres to go.

The weather and snow conditions were reasonable the entire week. The day we arrived at the summit was a gorgeous blue-sky day, but very cold. We didn't spend long at the top — just looked around us, took some pictures and headed down.

From the summit, we descended to the third camp at 5,182 metres. The cold temperatures had caused a crust to form on the snow that made travelling more difficult. We slept there for a couple of hours until the sun returned and the snow softened up.

The next day we travelled down the ridge, packing up and taking with us all of the remaining gear from each of the three camps. By midnight, we were off the mountain. In slightly more than twenty-four hours, with just a few hours sleep, we made it from the summit back to the base of the mountain.

At the time of that trip we didn't know anything about altitude sickness and that kind of stuff, so we didn't get it. We travelled fast enough that it couldn't catch us, I guess.

TOP On June 12, 1959, all six of us stood on the summit. BOTTOM The fact that the front points of our crampons didn't make it past the tip of the mukluks didn't bother us too much, as you can see. We couldn't ski with them but we couldn't ski well with the Kodiaks either.

Our only real problem was that missing bag of noodles from the airdrop. We had planned for rice and noodles to be the mainstay of our diet. So, with the noodles lost in a crevasse, we ate rice — rice soup, rice with sausages, rice with this, rice with that, and rice pudding for dessert. Every meal. For three weeks.

At base camp we had one day of rest.

On the trip out, we began down the East Logan Glacier again, and then onto the Hubbard Glacier. Once on the Hubbard, we changed course, returning via a different route than the way we came. This time, we travelled to the head of the Hubbard Glacier and down the Donjek Glacier.

On that return trip, each of us hit a breaking point at one time or another. Smylie, for instance, reached his on the second day after we left base camp. He was fed up, and for a day he just trudged along like a zombie. Then, at the head of the Donjek Glacier, Hans lost it. By this stretch of the trip, we were travelling by night (and slept in the day), because it was cooler then and the snow was a little harder, making the ice easier to move on. That evening Hans refused to get up. Normally, he was the one to shout and get everybody moving, but that night I had to say, "Hans, it's time to go," and he said, "Aw, I don't give a damn." He'd reached that point on the other side.

So I got things rolling, and we continued to descend once more. All of us were so tired and beyond caring by then that we travelled down the glacier un-roped and made some really dangerous moves. Finally, though, we reached the toe of the glacier, everyone intact.

The glacier was so broken up and full of crevasses near the toe that we had to retreat and travel on the edge moraine. After nearly three weeks on ice, we finally stepped back onto solid ground. In a little green meadow nearby, a rock rabbit hopped past, and a small stream meandered alongside the clearing. We immediately set up camp, collapsed there and slept for twenty-four hours.

Once off the glacier, we had little use for our skis anymore, but instead of dumping them, we were bound and determined to carry them all the way out. No matter what, we were going to return those skis back to the Head Ski Company. As it turned out, we were glad to have kept them — they came in handy for the rafts.

The next day, the plan was to find the airdropped dinghies, load them up, and raft down the Donjek River all the way to the Alaska Highway.

We had come off the ice on the north side. The Donjek Glacier actually ran across the valley, and the river, which started further up, ran underneath it for a distance. The ground at the base of the glacier was covered with really heavy underbrush — willows and alders that grew two to three metres high. Mosquitoes immediately swarmed us when we entered the area.

Despite searching for the dinghies for a quite a while in that underbrush, we couldn't find them. We finally realized they must have been dropped on the other side of the river by mistake. Being early June, the Donjek River was already moving fast due to spring runoff. Ice floes, which had broken off the glacier only a short distance above us, littered the stream.

It was decided that Hans and I would cross the river. From where we stood, there were three channels of water, two of which we could wade across. One, however, was too deep and fast to hold our footing. We would have to swim it.

Hans and I stripped down naked and threw our clothes in our backpacks. We waded across the first two channels of waist-deep water using ski poles for balance. Once on dry land again, we ran and jumped up and down to try to warm up. We put our clothes on for a short while, then took them off and went for it, this time having to swim. The water was deep and ice-cold. Large ice floes passed us by but luckily we were able to avoid getting hit by one. At one point, Hans disappeared under the water and didn't surface for a long time. I was really scared until I saw him suddenly pop up a ways down the river.

Once across this third channel, we searched for the dinghies for a long while before finding three of the four that had been airdropped for us. One of these was punctured in several places as a result of the fall from the plane, making it completely useless. The other two would have to do.

These rubber dinghies were inexpensive two-man rafts made in Japan, another one of our purchases from the army surplus store. We successfully inflated them and Hans jumped in one, I in the other. We rafted back to the guys, but not without incident. I hit some whitewater, and the dinghy rode over a wave and crashed hard on a rock, smashing my tailbone in the process. It hurt something terrible. That little souvenir from the trip caused me problems for almost a year afterwards.

Preparing the rafts.

On shore once again, we prepared everything to raft down the river the following day. That night, I reached *my* breaking point. When I woke the next morning, I walked up the river a ways. I was angry and tired, and didn't want to see anybody. In my mind I was thinking, "*If anybody says a word to me right now, I'll take a swing at him with my ice axe.*"

What had totally set me off was that the day before, when Hans and I had swum across the river and Hans had had his close call underwater, I looked over at the other guys once we made it to shore. There was one of them cutting his toenails. He didn't even look up to see if we had drowned. Obviously we were all exhausted and beyond the normal stage of caring, but that really pissed me off.

Another time I had problems with the same guy. As I unpacked my pack, out came some stuff that wasn't mine. All of a sudden this guy yells, "What you doing with my socks?" Well, I sure as hell didn't put his socks in my pack. I unknowingly carried his stuff up the hill for him and then he made it out like I had stolen it.

Anyway, we finally had the two rubber dinghies ready to go. Using the air mattresses we slept on and our skis, we decided to make two more rafts. We piled all the equipment on the new rafts and tied it down. Then we hung the equipment rafts behind each of the dinghies and started down the river, two of us in one raft and two in the other. The two left had to walk along the shore. One reason that the Head Ski Company had lent us the skis was to test them at high speeds. Well, the fastest those skis went on the entire trip was down that whitewater.

After rafting for a distance, Hans's raft was punctured. A ski had penetrated his dinghy and he had a flood right in the middle of the river. We made it to the side just in time, but the dinghy was useless. So we tied the two equipment rafts together to form one large raft and then tied that to the one remaining dinghy. Smylie and I rafted down, dinghy in the front and the large raft trailing behind — or at least that was the idea. None of us had much idea about river rafting.

The rest of the guys had to walk the remaining sixty-five kilometres out. Luckily, they found a mining road fairly early on, so the going got a lot easier for them and they made great time. The problem was we had run out of food by that point and were all very hungry.

The ride down the river for Smylie and me was really wild — and continued all day and night. We had very little control over the equipment raft since it was twice as heavy as we were. Sometimes it was in front of us and sometimes behind. There were places where the river had carved a path in underneath the permafrost. The permafrost was sticking out like a giant roof about six metres over our heads, with trees growing out of its frozen soil. We were beneath it in the rapids, flying by the driftwood, the rocks and everything else. At times, the raft would brush up against the bank under a huge overhang. As you can imagine, we were very happy when we finally saw the pylons of the old bridge on the Alaska Highway in the distance.

At the very last minute, within sight of the Alaska Highway, Smylie and I noticed one large snag sticking up out of the river. Somehow we navigated the dinghy past it, but the raft hooked on behind it and no matter what we did, we couldn't pry it loose. There was just too much water pressure. After trying for a long time, we cut the dinghy loose. We attempted a few times to carry the dinghy back above the raft, get in the water, ride it up against the thing and see if we could get the raft loose, but there was no way. Finally, we gave up and drifted down to the highway. The equipment raft remained hooked on that snag in the middle of the river.

We crawled out onto the highway and laid there for a while. I didn't even have boots or a jacket because everything was on the equipment raft.

Some tourists came by and stopped. We were extremely hungry, not having eaten anything since the start of our raft trip and having lived on mainly rice for the three weeks before that. So we asked them if they could they give us something to eat. The lady offered to make us ham sandwiches. She placed the ham on the buttered bread, but then proceeded to fumble and search around for what seemed like a very long time while we stood there desperately waiting.

Eventually, I asked, "Lady, what are you looking for?"

She said, "The mustard. I can't find the mustard."

In my head, I was screaming, "I don't need any damn mustard. I'm starving here. Just give me the fucking sandwich."

Of course, after I wolfed it down, I turned to the woman and politely said, "Thank you very much, ma'am. That was the best tasting sandwich ever."

Soon after we ate our lunch, a car came from the opposite direction carrying the other four guys. The night before, they had kept walking, eager to get back to civilization, and had arrived at the Alaska Highway at about two o'clock in the morning. They found a gas station and a restaurant on the highway nearby, but it was closed. Starving, they woke up the two old caretakers of the place who couldn't give them any restaurant food but offered to sell them snacks such as chocolate bars and potato chips from the store. Within a couple of hours, the guys had eaten eighty dollars worth of snacks, at a time when chocolate bars cost a nickel.

When we were all together, Smylie and I told them about the hooked raft. We decided to try to find a motorboat. At Burwash Landing, Grace Chambers lent us a boat, a motor and a pickup truck. Soon we were back on the river, headed upstream. There again was the raft, still stuck in the strong current, the snag sticking out and the whole thing tucked in behind it.

First we tried to get the equipment off the raft but couldn't. Then we decided that one of us would cut the rope that was holding the raft to the snag, but unfortunately when we did that the whole thing sort of exploded. Everything on the raft went down the river and sank. All we could catch was a couple of sleeping bags floating on top. The rest was all gone, including, by far our worst loss, most the photographs of our trip. One guy had been charged with looking after the pictures, but unbeknownst to the rest of us, he didn't want to carry them out and had instead put them in with the stuff on the raft. Luckily, a few photos survived and as well, Hans had carried the film from the movie he was making, so later we all made a set of slides off of that.

I don't think we ever did receive the additional $1,500 from the national newspaper, because of those missing photographs.

I lost more than two kilograms on that trip. That summer I went on to climb another sixty mountains in Jasper, Banff, Rogers Pass and the Bugaboos before the end of September. At that time I was in such good shape, a grizzly bear would have bitten his teeth out if he had attacked me.

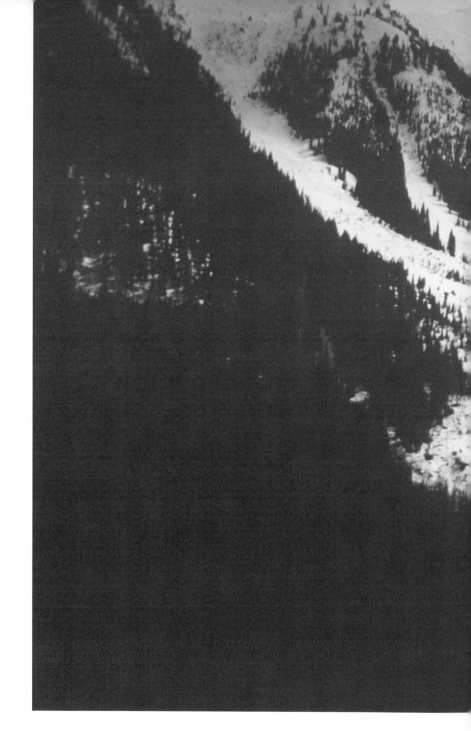

Tonnes of snow in motion, at speeds of more than 160 km/hr, Rogers Pass.

4

THE SIDEHILLGOUGER SAYS,

*"In an avalanche area, it is important to travel
spaced out — between the guys, I mean."*

IN 1960, I met my future wife, Anni, in Jasper. Like me, she had come to Canada from Austria to travel and see the world, with full intentions of eventually returning home. Anni, too, loved the mountains. She was a good skier and climber, and we went on a lot of great trips together and had a lot of fun. We fell in love and in 1961, we were married. Our three children, Susi, Fred and Eva, were born over the next several years.

Once I had a family, I became more concerned about the long-term future. My ski shop in Jasper was going reasonably well, but I was impatient and frustrated by what I saw as short-sightedness in the community. At that time, the only ski lifts in Jasper were on Whistlers Mountain, very near the town site. The slopes were low in altitude and that made the snow coverage very unpredictable. Sometimes rain ruined the slopes in the middle of winter. Many of us would go up to the much better slopes at Marmot Basin, but since there were no lifts we had to climb to get some runs in. There was talk in town of developing the Marmot Basin area, but the progress was very slow.

In 1963, I gave up waiting, sold my guiding business to Hans Schwarz and my store to someone else, and took a job running the ski school at the newly opened Big White Ski Area near Kelowna, British Columbia. The management there made some promises that weren't fulfilled, so the next season I moved on and worked in

Penticton, BC. At that point however, I already had my eye on a job with Parks Canada and was waiting for an opening.

A few years earlier, while still in Jasper, I had had the opportunity to take part in a warden training course at Cuthead Camp, thirty-five kilometres north of Banff, up the Cascade Valley. A guy named Walter Perren ran the course.

Based in Banff National Park, Walter Perren was the rescue specialist for all the mountain parks at the time. His official title was assistant chief warden, but he was really the first alpine specialist. In the several years that he had worked for Parks, he laid the initial foundation for mountain rescue and public safety. He had a huge job and a tough one. The wardens at that time were all cowboys, good at patrolling the backcountry on horseback. Walter had to try to turn them into mountaineers.

Anni.

Walter and I hit it off and he soon realized that with my mountaineering experience, I could help him. So shortly after I attended that first course, I started helping Walter instruct some of the summertime mountaineering and rescue courses for the wardens. I didn't have time to assist on courses in the winter because of ski coaching and running my ski shop. In addition to the courses, whenever a rescue came up in the Jasper area, Parks would hire me to take part. I really enjoyed those experiences and they deepened my interest in Parks Canada work.

I knew a full-time job would eventually come up with the government and I waited for it. In the summer of 1965, I got my chance. Parks had made some changes at Rogers Pass in Glacier National Park related to highway avalanche control and as a result, a job was advertised. I bid on it and … didn't get it. Another applicant for the position, who had taken part in a course I had taught the previous year, was hired. For completing that school (what we called the courses), he received a certificate, signed by me. Then he won the competition for the Parks job over me because he had a certificate and I didn't. That's the government for you!

Anyway, they corrected that turn of events afterwards and I landed the position. So Anni, the kids and I moved to Revelstoke, BC for a short period of time and then up to the avalanche research station near the top of Mount Fidelity in Rogers Pass.

Rogers Pass and Revelstoke are on the windward side of the mountains and thus receive some of the highest snowfalls in North America (an average of over nine metres per year). The winter we spent up on Fidelity had a record snowfall of thirty metres, almost six metres of which lay compacted on the ground by mid season.

The narrow pass discovered by Major A.B. Rogers in 1882, is bordered by the steep Selkirk Mountains on both sides, which make for numerous slide paths. The mountains in the Selkirk Range are heavily covered by massive spruce, hemlock and cedar trees, but in areas where there are no trees, or where trees have been knocked down by previous slides, the snow has nothing to anchor it.

Man and avalanches in the Rogers Pass area had a difficult beginning. The Canadian Pacific Railroad line through the pass

was completed in 1885, but for the first number of years it was shut down during the winter due to the extreme avalanche hazard. Thirty-one snow sheds totaling more than six kilometres in length were then built to protect the trains, but even this was not sufficient. In the period from 1885 to 1911, 236 people were killed by avalanches. The worst accident occurred on March 10, 1910, when fifty-eight men trying to clear the snow from one avalanche, were hit and killed by another that came down from a mountain on the opposite side of the valley. Eventually, CP Rail decided to go underground. They built the eight kilometre long Connaught Tunnel under Rogers Pass in 1916, which eliminated the biggest part of the exposure problem.

In Rogers Pass you quickly learned respect for nature.

The Trans-Canada Highway through Rogers Pass and Glacier National Park opened in 1962. This also marked the beginning of an avalanche control program that over time evolved into the largest program of its kind in the world. In 1965, Fred Schleiss was named chief avalanche forecaster for the highway and over the next twenty-six years, with the help of his brother, Walter and the Canadian Army set up and ran the extensive program. I was hired to assist him in those early days.

Soon people in charge of avalanche control programs around the world were coming to observe what we were doing in Rogers Pass. The chore of making sure that the highway was safe from avalanches was actually more difficult than for the railroad.

There are 132 slide paths in total between the town of Golden, BC, and Revelstoke. From the eastern to western Park boundary there are eighty-three known and mapped slide paths along the road. Seven snow sheds were installed to protect the road from the major slide paths; the rest is controlled by explosives. Over the years, more than ten million people have travelled that stretch of highway and to date, there have been only two fatalities caused by avalanches.

Working at Rogers Pass was a real experience for me because it gave me a chance to learn the scientific end of snow and avalanches. I had the feel for it, a gut instinct developed from years of travelling in the mountains, but before the Pass, I did not have the scientific knowledge.

I spent three years there and learned all the technical ins and outs of snow research and snow studies. I couldn't just phone down to the office and say, "I've got a bad feeling about the avalanche situation today. I think we should close the road." I could no longer base my decisions solely on a gut feeling. I had to use facts and figures. I learned that in Rogers Pass, in the three years I was there. I learned how avalanches are created and how to control them, how to do snow profiles, how to determine risk level and things like that. In a somewhat related but separate task we also studied how wolves and other animals behave in the winter in a place like Rogers Pass.

My job while I was there was almost entirely outside. I was responsible for visiting and checking the outlying snow stations, and completing snow profiles and readings, which had to be done on a weekly basis in an effort to determine the avalanche danger. This involved a lot of travel on skis in heavy snow, but I was

Several snow sheds protect motorists on the Trans-Canada Highway. Avalanches have come down from the mountains on both sides of the narrow valley.

 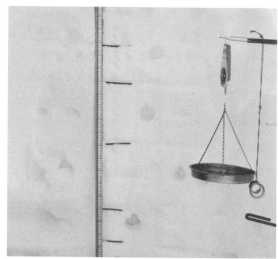

LEFT Conducting
a snow profile.
RIGHT Identifying
layers in the
snowpack.

lucky to have some good guys like Paul Peyto helping me. When returning from some of the high mountain snow stations, we had a lot of fun skiing the deep snow in the gullies there.

In addition to Fred Schleiss, I learned a lot from Peter Schaerer, head of the National Research Council's avalanche section. The three of us also travelled to Europe and the United States, where we attended various courses and saw what other places were doing in regards to snow safety.

The snowpack is a living thing. It changes from the time the snowflake begins falling through the air to the time that it melts on the ground months later. Metamorphism is always taking place within the snowpack, and is influenced by snow depth, density and temperature. Air temperature, direct sunshine on the snow surface, amount of radiation (which penetrates the snowpack), rain and wind velocity must also be observed in order to make accurate predictions of avalanche risk.

By continuously observing the condition of the snowpack, monitoring the weather, and estimating how the future weather may affect the stability of the snowpack on mountain slopes, one attempts to predict avalanche hazard.

Although avalanche hazard forecasters can evaluate the present stability of the snowpack from their own observations, they are dependent on a reliable weather forecast for making a prediction of the conditions for the near future. Such predictions of the avalanche hazard twenty-four to forty-eight hours in advance are necessary for making key decisions, such as closing roads and ski runs, canceling guided ski trips and helicopter flights, and scheduling avalanche control by artillery. Consequently, the accuracy of the avalanche hazard forecast affects the economics and the safety of personnel of public and private operations.

Avalanches generally fall into two categories — loose snow and slab. Loose snow avalanches start at a single point or over a small area, and initiate a chain reaction, thus growing in size as they descend.

Slab avalanches, on the other hand, start when a well-defined fracture line in the snow develops and a large area of snow begins to slide at once — as much as one million cubic metres can give way in an instant. Many things, including the weight of a skier, can trigger slab avalanches. When the added weight becomes greater than the resistance between snow layers below the surface, the snow slides. Slab avalanches are the greater hazard of the two.

In Rogers Pass we handled avalanches like hot buns. We shot them down. We had 132 slide paths to control, and at times we would shoot fifty avalanches down in one day, some of them major in size.

Fracture line of a slab avalanche.

The idea was that the snow research section (us) did the forecasting and then when the time came, we would instruct the Canadian army guys who were stationed at the Pass where and when to shoot the artillery to trigger a slide. We would aim into the snow at the top of an avalanche slope and if we did it right, the avalanche came down, preferably to the edge of the highway. That's how the control was done.

The army used a 105 Howitzer, which could shoot a maximum distance of 11,200 metres. Due to the 105 Howitzer's classification as a military combat weapon under the jurisdiction of the Canadian Army, no civilian, under any circumstances, was allowed to load or shoot it. Thus we worked in partnership in Rogers Pass.

Like I said at the beginning, not everything went right *all* of the time. Take for instance an avalanche we shot off of Mount Tupper one late winter day. We had shot an avalanche down at this location many times before, and it had always run the normal slide path off to the left.

The snow had all kinds of space to run in that direction, and it always did, so we parked our vehicles to the right of the slide to do our work. We shot up into the slope; it released and started coming down. All of a sudden, that day, it turned and came straight for us. I was suddenly standing in the middle of the slide path. Peter Schaerer was standing in a safe spot on top of the snow shed, taking pictures.

So there I was—the first Parks planner, deciding if I should save myself or the government property. I left the Parks vehicle, and ran up the road to where a large army truck was parked. I just had time to dive in underneath that truck and hang onto the rear axle when the avalanche struck. The impact of the avalanche pushed that (very heavy) army truck several metres down the road. Snow flowed everywhere, including under the truck where I was hanging, but I was okay.

When it was all over, the government vehicle was completely demolished. You can imagine the force that vehicle was hit with. We thought the only safe place would have been in the glove compartment.

The first winter that my family and I lived in Rogers Pass, we were stationed at the Fidelity Mountain snow station. We spent the winter high up on the mountain, accessible only by snowcat, snowmobile or skis.

A 105 Howitzer.

Normally the slide would veer off to our left. Don't you believe it, that a civil servant can't make a quick decision!

Our house was on two-and-a-half metre stilts. By mid-winter, the windows were completely covered and the snow reached the roofline.

Living on Mount Fidelity was a great time for the family. Fredy and Susi were young, only three and four years old. We lived in a house that was perched on two-and-a-half-metre stilts, but even so it was almost buried by snow in mid-winter. That was the year with almost six metres of compacted snow on the ground. It was good planning that the front door opened inward, because some mornings we awoke to a wall of snow that I had to shovel up and out in order for us to leave the house. I shoveled out the kitchen window, too, so we had some natural light in the house. The kids loved to climb up the steep roof and slide down in front of the kitchen window, getting a bit of a drop as they went.

A lot of times we were above the weather on Fidelity. We were in the sunshine and down below it would be snowing. It was tough to get the six kilometres down to the highway with the kids though. If conditions were reasonable, they would ski down the cat track.

We loved it up at Fidelity, but after that first winter, the powers that be decided that we should move down into the community at Rogers Pass. There were about ten families living there at the time.

While in Rogers Pass, Anni knitted me the first of many pairs of knicker socks. At the time, standard climbing gear consisted of knickers and long woolen socks that reached up to your knees. I found it very difficult to find a pair of socks that fit me well — they were all too tight in the calves. So Anni made me a beautiful pair with lots of cables, designed to fit perfectly. She used bright red wool. From then on I wore red socks.

Anni and I.

Years later, the standard issue socks given to the wardens for rescue work were grey. I always told the guys that only *alpine specialists* were allowed to wear red socks. It started off as a joke, but the red socks became more and more serious over time. Nobody would dare to wear red socks to a school or a climb I was conducting, and if new recruits accidently showed up in some, they were given a hard time — by the other guys.

During those years in Glacier National Park, Anni and I would often leave the kids with a babysitter and go climbing on my days off. The mountains around there were beautiful, many were challenging and we climbed just about every one of them. Because we were well organized and prepared, we never ran into trouble, which made for many fantastic days but not many memorable stories.

I worked in Rogers Pass for three years. In the summertime, my duties included signing out and advising climbers about routes in the area, as well as assisting the wardens with various seasonal tasks. I was stationed at Glacier National Park, but I took part in rescues when they arose in various western Canadian mountain parks.

I also continued to instruct regional warden schools in climbing and rescue skills for Walter Perren. By that time, Walter Perren had a few wardens with a base of knowledge in climbing, skiing and rescue in place, who together formed the first national parks rescue team.

Sadly, Walter Perren developed leukemia and in 1967, he died. He was only fifty-three years old and was survived by a wife and three sons. That spring, due to his illness, they asked me to fill in for him. We moved the whole family to Banff. Just before Walter died, I saw him and he said, "You take the job. Nobody else has a chance. You have got all the mountaineering experience, the qualifications for blasting and knowledge of the situation."

Later, a competition for his job came up and I… didn't get it. The Parks plan, though, was for me to train the guy who did.

I placed third in the competition. Peter Fuhrmann won the position and Fred Schleiss came in second. Afterwards Parks realized that was maybe not quite the right choice, because Fuhrmann really didn't have the kind of experience needed for the job in regards to snow, avalanches and rescues. With some wrangling, they decided to split the position in two. They offered me the second job and stationed me in Jasper. Peter was stationed in Banff and Fred Schleiss returned to running the Rogers Pass avalanche program.

Peter and I couldn't have been more different, but in spite of the rough start to our partnership, it turned out that we actually made a great team. He had a lot of political savvy and was able to schmooze up to the right people, getting us the money, equipment and contacts we needed. I spent more time out in the field, training, testing and building. We had a lot of trust in each other. At times over the years, management tried to turn us against one another but never succeeded.

I stayed in Banff for a few months after I got the job, to start up the avalanche control program there. Coming fresh out of the snow business in Rogers Pass, I was shocked to see that in Banff National Park not a single weather station had been set up along the roads or at the three alpine ski areas to help forecast avalanche conditions. There were no avalanche control methods of any sort in use either. In fact, the only thing I noticed had been set up at the time was some trip wires on the Sunshine Ski Area road. I don't know what their purpose was, because if an avalanche tripped the wires, it was certainly too late to do anything.

With the help of the wardens, we established snow study stations where necessary. Most of them are still in use today. We put some equipment in place for the following winter. I started to make an atlas of avalanche paths on the Sunshine road and the Icefields Parkway, then numbered and named them. A basic set-up was in place before the next winter.

Then my family and I moved back to Jasper. We had come full circle. And it was great to be back.

Peter and I were given the official title of Alpine Specialist. Our job description called for everything from packhorse to public speaker. We were on the staff of the Calgary Regional Office of Parks Canada and our boss was Jimmy Sime.

I was responsible for Jasper, Revelstoke, Glacier and Waterton National Parks in Canada, and Glacier Park in Montana. Soon afterwards Kluane and Nahanni National Parks were established in the north and added to my list. The wardens and I also helped with rescues in BC's Mount Robson Provincial Park when required.

Montana's Glacier Park and Canada's Waterton National Park were part of an international peace park. As part of this, it was agreed that Waterton would look after the public safety training and rescue work for both parks, while Glacier was responsible for fire suppression training for both parks.

Peter was responsible for Banff, Yoho and Kootenay Parks, which together had by far the largest number of visitors of all the national parks, as well as Pacific Rim. Once the northern parks were established, Peter and I were responsible for mountain rescue and public safety in an area larger than the size of Switzerland.

Several of the parks are largely undeveloped; access was, and still is, difficult. The mountains were largely composed of decaying sedimentary rock, which adds more danger for climbers and mountaineers, and there are extensive glaciers and icefields. The weather is unpredictable and complex. We had a big job.

The idea was that the wardens would perform the rescues and deal with public safety issues as they arose. Peter and I had to provide the warden staff with the necessary means to do so (equipment, training, technology). It was essential that the wardens knew their parks. Actually, the original idea was that our job would be to sit there in the office and write nice memos to all the parks to tell them how they should set up their safety program and what they should do to train the wardens. But that's not the way I saw it.

Originally, with Walter Perren, one rescue school a year had been set up to teach the entire warden service. Candidates from each park could attend. I immediately set up yearly winter and summer schools in each of the parks I was responsible for.

Over time, the job became even broader. I also began to train the RCMP dog masters in avalanche rescue. I did not train the dogs. The dogs were trained in Innisfail, Alberta by their masters, but I trained the team to arrive at an accident site safely and to survive once they were there.

Years before, in 1963, I was one of the founding members of the Association of Canadian Mountain Guides (ACMG). I continued my involvement in the association as an examiner of guide candidates.

In 1981, I was part of the founding group of the Canadian Avalanche Association. Contact with this group also continued throughout my career.

Nobody really knew much about avalanches and snow then, so Peter Schaerer of the National Research Council and I started running snow and avalanche courses for the public and various interest groups.

We also became involved with heli-skiing. There was an accident in Valemount, BC, where thirty-two people were caught in an avalanche that resulted in one fatality and one person losing an eye. At the inquest that followed, I recommended that the operators should have a lease of occupation for a given group of mountains. Each operation could then map its area, get to know

WILL YOU BE THE NEXT
AVALANCHE VICTIM ?

R.O.Wood

REDUCE THE ODDS

CONSULT THE SNOW SAFETY WARDEN
FOR THIS AREA BEFORE VENTURING
FROM THE RECOGNIZED SKI RUNS

the hazards within it, and study the snow conditions. They would also not be chasing each other for fresh snow. That system is still in place today.

Later on, a similar thing happened with snowmobilers when an avalanche, also in Valemount, killed four people. We gave recommendations again on what should be done and again they were followed up.

Peter Fuhrmann originated helicopter and sling-rescue operations in Canada and I started the first pilot testing for these.

We also held Parks ski guides examinations and continued to help with the guiding examinations for the ACMG.

After the Trans-Canada Highway was built over Rogers Pass (1962), the Yellowhead Highway was built further north, as was the Icefields Parkway from Banff to Jasper, and the Kootenay Highway to Radium. All of these roadways needed avalanche control, which Peter Fuhrmann or I set up.

Several alpine ski areas in the parks required avalanche control systems as well, which we also set up and ran.

Everything was in its beginning stages and we had our fingers in almost every pie. Later when many of our avalanche control programs were in place, others followed what we started. I am well satisfied with what we accomplished both in and outside the national parks system.

An early avalanche awareness poster.

Mount Edith
Cavell.

5

THE SIDEHILLGOUGER SAYS,

"Willi hasn't fallen on skis since 1967.
Anything after that was done purely for
research purposes."

MOUNTAIN RESCUE IN CANADA is now highly sophisticated, but when I started it was anything but. Walter Perren had a huge job developing some basic climbing knowledge in the wardens and setting up a program from scratch.

When I started running courses for Walter in the early 1960s, specialized equipment wasn't often available, so we used what we could find and improvised a lot. In fact, improvisation discussions and exercises were a part of every training school we held.

Helmets, for example were not regularly used by climbers at that time, so we had difficulty finding any to buy. We decided to use construction hard hats, which led to some interesting situations.

Once I was leading a school in Yoho National Park. One of the wardens taking the course had this large, unusually-shaped head. We were practicing rescue techniques on a rock face, our heads protected by the hard hats. Suddenly a rock came flying down from above and hit this guy right on the top of the helmet. Construction helmets have an iron band inside that is covered with leather. The outer shell is of course plastic. The rock hit the plastic shell, causing it to splinter and fly off in all directions. Although the helmet did protect his head from injury, the impact of the rock drove the iron band down over his big head. It came to rest around his eyes. Try as we may, we couldn't get the band off.

He wasn't in pain but couldn't see a thing. We had to lead him down the mountain and to a hospital, where the doctors managed to cut it off somehow.

During Walter's time, we trained the wardens in two gigantic camps a year — one in the summer and one in the winter. Wardens from all the mountain parks congregated in one spot. Most of the camps went off without a hitch, but I remember a very close call one summer while conducting a rescue school at Rogers Pass. We climbed a distance up onto McDonald Ridge above a steep but not vertical face, and were going to practice lowering a guy down in one of the old metal stretchers (a mine basket) we used at the time. The stretcher was attached to a two-and-a-half-millimetre cable.

We tied one warden into the stretcher and then a teammate guided it down the mountain in front while a few other guys fed the cable down from above. On the slope below the stretcher was a rock slab, and halfway down the slab was an upturned tree root. It was the only tree that had ever grown on that exposed place, but some years before it had died and fallen over, trunk pointing down the slope. The circle of roots, about two metres in diameter, was just perched there on that slab.

All of a sudden, the cable broke. The stretcher and the two guys, one in the stretcher and the other one leading it, went tumbling down the slope, ass over teakettle. As luck would have it, they ended up behind that upright tree root, the only one on the whole mountain slope, and it stopped them. Otherwise it would have been a long way down.

The only resulting injury was the tip of an ice axe speared the lip of the warden in the stretcher making a hole right through it. Actually, the guy's name was Pierce.

We started all
this out with
mine baskets
and ropes.

He was really shaken up. So I put Gord Peyto in charge of the rest of the team and I took him down. Gordy gathered up the equipment and got everybody else off the mountain. The whole crew was a little rattled by the incident, so taking Pierce away from the scene helped remove some of the pressure everyone felt.

When I first stepped into the alpine specialist position in the late sixties, there was an explosion of interest in climbing, backcountry skiing and other outdoor activities. All of a sudden, a lot of people started going into the mountains, most with very little knowledge of mountain safety. It was like a match had been lit and almost immediately we had a brush fire.

For the most part, these new adventurers were young people with no background in mountaineering, no information passed down from the older generation, and very few sources from which to gain mountain skills.

Cross-country skiing had become very popular, and not knowing the alternatives, people began using the lightweight boots, skis and bindings for almost any mountain excursion, from climbing high peaks to crossing glaciers. The equipment was not designed for this, so naturally, it caused all kinds of trouble, including broken equipment and frozen feet, stranding skiers in the backcountry. Our job came just at the right time.

One time, a group of us were on the top of Mount Columbia, the highest mountain in Alberta. Below, we saw two guys hoof it across the entire Columbia Icefields dressed like they were going fishing, wearing little rucksacks to carry their lunch, and with light cross-country equipment on. Luckily for them, the weather held and they had their track to follow back, so they were in and out in a day. But numerous accidents happened due to lack of preparation for changing weather or snow conditions. Some fell in crevasses, or they became hypothermic.

One rescue in 1972 occurred when a party of five ventured out onto the Columbia Icefields unroped. One member of the group fell into a crevasse, as they were skiing up the second headwall of the Athabasca Glacier. The best route through the crevasses of the second headwall was along the northwest side of the Athabasca Glacier. However, the overhanging Dome Glacier presented a very real threat of icefall or avalanche from above, and therefore it was always important to move through that area as quickly as possible.

The climbing party was the first one out on the glacier that day, so following the accident a number of other groups caught up to them and were trying to help with the rescue. As a result, when our rescue team arrived on site, forty people were underneath the active Dome Glacier. Our first action was to clear the area and to make sure all persons were roped up.

The victim had been pulled out of the crevasse by that point. He had been attended to and declared dead by a medical doctor who was a member of one of the climbing parties. Not wanting to spend too much time in that area ourselves, we worked quickly to move the body to the lower glacier using a portable toboggan. He was then taken by Skidoo and snowcat to the highway.

Following the rescue, we reflected on the lack of safe practices we had observed:

> *the party was unroped on the glacier*

> *the party intended to cross a major icefield and climb a high mountain in light cross country racing equipment*

> *the absolute beginner of the group was sent down the glacier alone to get help, after one accident had already occurred*

> *forty people were assembled underneath the active Dome Glacier for up to three hours*

Obviously more education about glacier travel was required. It was clear that very few people knew much about avalanches either, and that there was very little information out there in the form of courses or books for people to access. Peter Schaerer was working for the National Research Council, and its mandate was to make knowledge available. So between the two of us, we took it upon ourselves to do something. We started avalanche courses to instruct people in snow science, avalanche precautions and rescue. These courses immediately caught on. The demand was huge. During our second year of running these courses for example, we decided to put on a session in Whistler, BC. More than sixty people signed up almost immediately, forcing us to cut off registration. For this type of training, sixty people are just too many to handle. Soon after that, we turned the whole thing over to BCIT (British Columbia Institute of Technology). We ran some courses for instructors and the institute took over training the public. In time, these evolved into the first Canadian Avalanche Association courses.

When I was stationed in Rogers Pass, working on winter avalanche control, I continued to run summer training schools in Banff. One of my frustrations at that time was that the wardens did not have equipment issued to them. They had a standard Parks street uniform, but that was it — not even a rucksack. I remember one Sunday afternoon there was a severe thunderstorm. A lot of climbers were signed out on various routes that day, and sure enough, the following morning, three registered parties had not returned. I started to get some wardens together to go out and look for the overdue climbers. The wardens had to go home and dress in whatever outdoor clothes they had. When they came back to the Parks office, I started doling out rescue equipment — rucksacks, pitons and hammers.... I alone had to think of everything, at a tense time when we were in a hurry to begin a search. It was a waste of time, and if I had forgotten something it could have affected the whole operation.

As we were preparing the victim for
transport, another party moved through.
They were roped up — but how?!
The second party was roped together
too closely, with no preparation made for
the arrest of a possible fall. Only one ice
axe was visible — on the first guy.

When I started the alpine specialist job, I thought this had to change right now. There was some money available, so I immediately outfitted every warden with the personal gear needed for mountain rescue, like appropriate boots, packs, clothes, and rock and glacier gear. When a warden was called out to a rescue, the equipment was packed, functional and ready to go.

Besides rescue equipment, in those early years we focused on training the wardens and providing public information. As time went by, we worked hard on improving our methods and ideas, as well as developing or adopting new ones.

The concept behind the training was that if you want to help someone else, you first have to know how to survive yourself. Wardens learned how to manage themselves in every mountain circumstance. If you had been trained as a team in forty below, then you would know how to manage that temperature on a rescue. After all, rescue work is about the team. My job was to provide team members with a means to do their job; that is, to provide training, equipment, technology and local knowledge so that they could successfully complete any rescue.

Training was a never-ending process. Annual refresher courses were held for a week at a time. At the entry level, large groups of wardens took part in classroom lectures and demonstrations in the early morning and late evenings, while spending most of the day out on the rocks and ice.

I stressed the importance of technique to the wardens. Muscling their way up a mountain or through difficult winter terrain using their strength and endurance would only get the young guys so far. Sooner or later, I would tire them out enough to get them to realize that they had to use technique to keep up to me.

Demonstrating how to lower a casualty in a carrying seat.

At the beginning, I felt as if I was holding up the whole roof, but over time, with training, more and more guys were helping me hold up that roof. Eventually, I didn't have to hold it at all any more. The wardens in each of the parks did it themselves. They could pull off a full rescue on their own.

Wardens of the mountain rescue teams in the various national parks were on call every day of the year on a twenty-four-hour basis. When not involved in a rescue, they would perform their regular warden duties.

Not all wardens were willing or able to perform mountain rescues, but almost everyone could contribute in one way or another. Some, for example, were very good at organizing equipment in the rescue room, a much-needed task to ensure efficient rescue response.

As the years went by, more and more females became a valuable part of the warden service and rescue team. One of these was Dianne Volkers, who we all called Lady Di. She was really good at her job — in skiing and with the horses and in everything she undertook. Stationed in Kootenay National Park, she took part in a number of rescues there.

We were always in three-person teams on a rope and I often had Lady Di join my team. We had some really outstanding trips. On winter ski touring trips, we sometimes arrived at iffy hills — slopes where there was avalanche concern. After assessing the situation, I would always ski down these slopes first, partly because of the gut feelings I had. Several times, I let her ski down the almost untracked powder first after me, which in those days, the wardens considered kind of an honour.

In the early '70s, Peter Fuhrmann introduced helicopter rescue to the rescue team, which brought a major change to the way we did things. This method of mountain rescue was adopted from the Europeans, and it meant that wardens could reach accident scenes more quickly. He and I were both involved in testing and perfecting its applications for our situation.

Rescuing someone off a mountain with the assistance of an aircraft was pioneered by the famous Swiss pilot, Herman Geiger. He landed his Piper Cub on a small snow patch on the side of a mountain, loaded up the injured person and then flew the patient to safety, saving the rescue team hours of dangerous and backbreaking work. Later, Herman Geiger lost his own life when he was involved in a mid-air collision with one of his students. Geiger's work was carried on by Dr. Fritz Buehler, who formed the "Swiss Air Rescue Services" and introduced the use of helicopters. In many cases, the speed of the operation and the smoothness of the evacuation saved the patient's life.

The system was simple and effective. It required a helicopter with plenty of power, and a flight ceiling of at least 3,500 metres. Early on, we used the Bell Jet Ranger 206B, operated by a top-notch pilot who was knowledgeable about mountain flying. An eighteen metre cable was attached to the helicopter's frame. Also required were a special helicopter rescue seat and a fully equipped rescue person with a stretcher. Naturally, this set-up had to be approved by the Ministry of Transport. The rescue person suspended under the helicopter was flown to the accident site or as nearby as possible.

As time went on and we became more comfortable with the method, we experimented with the cable length. In situations where almost vertical walls did not allow enough clearance for the rotor blades, extensions were added to the top of the cable to make it up to thirty metres long.

The idea was that you tied yourself to a cable on the underside of the helicopter and then flew to the accident site. At the site, you did your thing. Then you called the helicopter back, hooked yourself and the loaded stretcher into the rope, and flew away to safety. Radio communication was necessary between the pilot and rescuer and the team member(s) on the ground.

Very soon after we adopted this method, we saved the lives of three people who probably otherwise would not have made it. Helicopter rescue became a quick system of fairly gentle transport that reduced search times from hours to minutes.

When we first decided to adopt the helicopter-sling method, we went from park to park to try it out and practice. Often there were a number of very reluctant looking wardens at the back of the group. At first, the pilots were not quite prepared for this type of flying either. Some of them took to it; some didn't even want to try.

Many people thought we were crazy. One look at an old JP helicopter tells you why — it just didn't have much power. For our purposes, the pilot took the door off and leaned out so he could see us hanging beneath the machine. No helmets and the use of an old radio. That's how we started. Nothing to it really.

Actually, it may look simple but it wasn't. It took a lot of practice. When I look back at the many pilots we tried this with (some great and some not so much), and the dumb things we did, I wonder how any of us made it. I know now though, after all the training and various methods we tried, that if there is an accident in helicopter rescue, then it would be a legitimate one.

Still, there were always the shadows of the unknown. One summer when we first used helicopters, we hauled a fellow off the almost vertical east face of Mt. Sorrow, approximately 500 metres above the valley bottom. With the old-fashioned cable rescue gear, this would have been a very hazardous and time-consuming job. We estimated it would have taken twenty men a day and a half to succeed. So we took a chance with a pilot who we knew was an excellent flier, but had never flown the sling-rescue method. To be honest, at that point we were not all that knowledgeable about it either. We had done a few rescues using the method, but still had a thing or two to learn.

Hans Fuhrer and Abe Loewen had already reached the scene of the accident by climbing up the rock face, and were applying first aid to the badly injured climber. (Thankfully, his climbing partner was okay). It was almost dark when the helicopter arrived. After giving a few simple instructions on the ground to the pilot and attaching the sling, a metal stretcher and myself to the cable beneath the helicopter, we took off to pick up the injured climber.

Several hundred feet above ground, the empty stretcher and I began to spin. I tried to counteract by shifting the stretcher, but by then the machine had picked up forward speed. The stretcher and I were left behind in the wash of the propeller. I started to spin at a terrific clip, round and round and round. Finally, the spinning came to a halt. I called down to Max, who was on the rock wall with the injured climber, to tell the pilot to go down. I was worried that the cable would over rotate and break. Nobody heard me. We were flying at an elevation of approximately 1,000 metres above the ground, and then the cable started to back spin.

Transporting a
rescue victim.

I became so dizzy dancing the tango up there. Imagine how I felt. I don't know why, but I crawled into the stretcher and just lay there, continuing to spin like crazy first in one direction, then in the other. One time when the cable had spun out to one side and stopped for a few seconds, I was close enough to the guys on the cliff face that they caught me by the arm. I unhooked myself and the stretcher from the helicopter and secured myself to the cliff wall. Once I had steadied myself, the three of us loaded the guy into the stretcher. We evacuated the injured climber and his partner without a hitch. Another day, another dollar.

From that incident, we learned that you could not fly a metal stretcher empty in a horizontal position. You had to fly it vertically; otherwise it could make for serious trouble. Another classic example of how we learned as we went along. This no longer was an issue later on when we began using fabric rather than metal stretchers.

During that rescue, we also had one of our first experiences with post-traumatic stress syndrome with the rescuers. Nobody knew the name for such a reaction in those days. But once we rescued the two climbers off the mountain, we flew back up with the helicopter and two extra harnesses to get Hans and Abe. These two guys were strong climbers and very able rescuers. They had practiced getting into the harness several times and had flown under the helicopter before. Up there that evening, neither one of them could find his way into that harness. I had one of them standing in front of me. I was holding the harness and I explained in detail how to get into it, but there was no way. Eventually it became too dark to continue to fly and the helicopter had to land. Hans and Abe had to spend the night up on the mountain.

The next day, I went up there at six o'clock in the morning and they were already down. They had had a miserable night.

Things like that happened many times. The guys would pull off a perfect rescue, adrenalin pumping, but then when the pressure was off, they would have problems performing some of the simplest tasks.

I felt really uneasy about some of the rescue pilots in the beginning, so I established a testing procedure for each of them. The first test we ran at Medicine Lake in Jasper National Park with seven pilots. Some failed and some passed. The testing procedure is fully accepted now, and to date, there hasn't been a single accident with the pilots.

Then came the rescue dogs. I had seen dogs be used in avalanche work in Europe and decided to try it. Our first dog was Ginger, a German shepherd with some coyote blood who did some really good work for us.

In 1971, Ginger was the only dog in North America trained in avalanche rescue. Warden Alfie Burstrom was the dog master, and worked hard with Ginger to teach him to search and track in an avalanche situation. As a team, they practiced a lot in order to keep the dog sharp and ready.

To help with practices, many of us would take turns being buried under several inches of snow. Ginger and Alfie would stand a good distance away. Then Alfie would give Ginger the signal and the dog would get busy finding us. Every time Ginger found one of us in the snow though, he would want to lick us all over. Maybe he thought we weren't clean enough.

Ginger also practiced locating buried articles of clothing — even buttons. Much to their credit, Alfie and Ginger became full-time members of the rescue team. This made Ginger the only civil servant in Canada who didn't drink coffee.

Ginger was incredibly smart. During one training session a number of years after Ginger joined our team, we had eight young police dogs and their trainers out in Bald Hills. It was a very cold day. We had buried ten pieces of moose hide in the snow a couple of days earlier in order for the scent to wear off a bit, but hopefully not so much that the dogs couldn't find them. We sent the police dogs out to look for the hides first, and after some time, two were able locate a hide each. The other eight dogs never even found one. Later that day, when we had all returned to the warden office, I asked Alfie to go out to the site with Ginger to see if he could locate the hides. I didn't want to leave them there — they were litter after all. Ginger found the remaining eight hides in a few short minutes.

One thing we learned from our experiences with Ginger was that Alfie had Ginger outside all the time, which made him ready to work at any time. Ginger would ride on the back of the pickup truck and sleep outside. Other rescue dogs were often kept inside heated cars and at night they were brought into houses. When they went out in the winter for long periods of time, it was like a person going out without a jacket. When they were put on a job, they were just not ready due to the cold.

Ginger located the bodies of many avalanche victims, but he was never on the scene fast enough to find someone alive. Nonetheless, his speed at a rescue site was legendary. In 1977, for example, a skier was caught in an avalanche above Hilda Creek Youth Hostel. The accident occurred at about 4:15 p.m. At 4:40 we were notified and called out. When Alfie arrived on the scene at 5:50 p.m., Ginger found the body of the victim within twenty seconds of being sent out to search. The skier was no longer alive.

Alfie made a harness to use with Ginger to fly under the helicopter. This was a first in Canada and around the world. The Europeans and Americans later copied Alfie's harness for their dogs. Ginger did well hanging under the helicopter, even for his first time. It was not much of a thing. We put him in the harness, hooked him and Alfie to the cable and off they flew. That was that. Alfie had a calm attitude about it and this translated to the dog.

In the summer, Ginger worked searching for lost people, locating river-drowning victims and also sometimes assisting in tracking down suspects in dope and arson cases.

I remember looking for a woman who had fallen into Maligne Canyon and was presumably drowned. Alfie and I headed for the Sixth Bridge, located a distance down from the canyon, just before the place where the Maligne River empties into the Athabasca. We planned to look for the woman between the Fifth and Sixth Bridges, but Ginger kept wanting to go down to the Athabasca rather than up toward the Fifth Bridge. Alfie wondered out loud, "What the hell do you want to go over there for?" but eventually let him go. More than a hundred feet down the trail beside the river totally submerged in water and hung up on a sweeper was the body of the woman we were looking for. Ginger had picked up her scent from the start. We had many dogs over the years but none were as good as Ginger.

Ginger
(with Alfie) in
his helicopter
harness.

In those early years another thing we did was join the International Commission for Mountain Rescue (ICAR). This organization was mainly made up of Europeans at the time; sixteen nations in total. We took a lot from them but we also contributed a great deal.

With the European countries, pride sometimes stood in the way. The Austrians would develop a good piece of equipment and the Swiss would refuse to use it, or vice versa. Instead they would develop their own prototype — something slightly different from the original piece.

We had no such qualms. We just took the best ideas and equipment from everyone, and then modified it to our situation. For example, one year the Swiss developed a net for under the helicopter — something to replace the metal stretcher. It was very nice but had a few small disadvantages. There was no way the Austrians were going to use that net, so they developed an enclosed sack named the Jenny Bag (after its inventor). So we put the Swiss net in the corner and took the sack. Then we discovered that we had slightly bigger and taller people in North America, plus due to the colder climate here, we wanted to be able to fit a sleeping bag inside the sack. So we had the thing made a little bit bigger. ICAR agreed with all this. If somebody developed something, they did not hold the patent or anything. So when we took an idea and changed it, no one would go after us for it.

We contributed our fair share, too. For example, when a person fell into a crevasse on a glacier, his fall stopped at the point where the crevasse narrowed. A long free fall could really jam him in there. It first, when the body was warm, it melted a little of the ice surrounding it and when the person's body cooled, the ice refroze. During a rescue or recovery, we had to chop him loose. Down there in that narrow hole, in the dark, we could hardly move. At first an ice axe was the only tool we had to chop the solid ice away and get the person loose. This was large and awkward for such a confined space. If your swing was inaccurate, you could poke a hole in the guy. (Most of the time, the victim was dead, but not always, so we had to be careful.) In response, we developed a chisel that we could use in a very confined area without harming anyone. This, too, was accepted by ICAR.

We developed some smaller pieces as well — a cable breaking device, a warning device when the cable was overstretched, and some other safety features related to the helicopter cable.

Later on, as we became involved in more specific rescue situations as well as some of the high altitude climbs in the St. Elias Mountains, if appropriate gear for our needs was not available, I designed it myself. This included various changes to sleeping bags, boots and bivvy sacs. In Canada, when we needed equipment or a new system, we would try out what was available. If it worked, we adopted it. If it didn't work, we threw it out and developed what we needed. Maybe I should have kept my ski shop — it could have evolved into a nice rescue gear business.

The joy
of snow.

6

THE SIDEHILLGOUGER ASKS,

*"Have you learned all of the different ways to
turn your skis? Right and left."*

WHEN YOU WATCH those cute, fluffy little snowflakes falling from the sky you can't imagine that they could ever do anybody any harm. When they accumulate though, they can cause several different hazards to mountain travellers, both in winter and summer.

A snow patch in the summer landscape is always a promise for some fun, but more people have come to harm sliding down one of those snow patches than you could imagine. Usually it looks harmless enough that an unprepared hiker will simply walk across a patch of snow. Then he slips, falls and starts to slide down. Now, how will he stop himself? With his fingernails? If the slope levels off or the snow is soft, then lucky for him, but usually it is the other way around — the slope steepens and the snow hardens. On the accident report under "cause of injury" it inevitably reads, "He entered the boulder field below the snow patch with excessive speed."

In the winter, nothing looks as harmless and is as treacherous as a patch of snow on the side of a mountain. If the snow is hard, there is the chance of slipping; if the snow is soft, it can avalanche. One should always cross a snow patch with caution and awareness of the terrain below. If there is no real danger, you can simply carry something for balance and brakes. If there is a cliff below, an ice axe must be used and a rope is necessary for belay.

Cornices are another danger. They result when the wind causes snow to drift over a mountain ridge, forming a kind of hanging roof. At first, a cornice grows straight out from the crest of the ridge top, but as time goes on the outside lip begins to settle and curl under.

The obvious hazard to the mountaineer is that these cornices fall off every so often. The cause of the break is similar to that of an avalanche: over-weighting of the cornice by additional snow, rain, or a person walking on it from the ridge. Changing temperature also weakens the bond between snow layers, and can cause a cornice to break off.

Travelling underneath a cornice is a calculated risk at any time, and travelling on top of cornices should be avoided at all cost. (The chance of over-weighting it with a person's own bulk is high, no matter how firm the snow looks.) Careful route-finding comes into play.

In areas of heavy snowfall, such as the Northern Selkirks, a second type of cornice is common. For a climber accustomed to Rocky Mountain conditions, this can be a real pitfall. Although they appear similar, these "snow ridges" are actually not true cornices, but rather are formed during the spring warm-up in places where a slab avalanche has broken away a short distance below the ridge. The thickness of the slab fracture can be anywhere from two to five metres. The remaining wall of snow is then exposed to the influence of air, temperature changes, radiation and an accelerated rate of metamorphism (the continuous changing process of individual snow grains within the snowpack). The updraft keeps chewing away at the wall and eventually hollows it out from underneath, forming a curl or cornice. The unfortunate climber who walks along this harmless-looking ridge from above, unprepared, will never know what hit him.

A cornice — the whole thing looks
like an overgrown donut.

A number of years back, we had an extended search for a single climber in the Rogers Pass area. During the fifth day of the search, we found footsteps onto one of those snow ridges and then a large section of ridge missing. We found some equipment a thousand metres below on the glacier. There was also a bottomless bergschrund where the glacier had moved away from the vertical rock of the mountain. A continuous hail of rocks, ice, snow and water came down from the face above into this grisly hole. After spending time assessing the situation, I came to the conclusion that it was not worth risking another life to look for the lost climber's remains. We abandoned recovery attempts. The reason it took us five days to find the guy was because the accident had occurred three mountains away from the original destination that the climber had signed out for.

It is important that winter travel equipment match the activity that it is meant for. I only used my cross-country ski equipment (narrow skis and light boots) for running at the valley bottom, mainly on designated trails. If I travelled above timberline or went on an overnight trip, I used ski touring equipment. The criteria I set for equipment was: a) it must be reliable and b) it must be functional under a wide variety of conditions.

Safety lies in the traveller's experience. A mechanical device can assist safety but cannot substitute for experience. Styles and fads can be disregarded for this purpose.

Another hazard of winter travel is the cold. If backcountry travellers become excessively chilled for some reason and cannot warm themselves up again or/and reach shelter, they risk frostbite or hypothermia.

Frostbite results when specific parts of the body, most commonly the fingers and toes, are exposed to the cold to the point that they freeze. When faced with extreme cold, the human body responds by protecting its inner core. It restricts blood flow to the skin surface in an effort to keep the core warm, but this action makes the extremities like fingers and toes more susceptible. A mild case of frostbite turns the skin white, numb and soft to the touch and can be treated on the spot. When it becomes more severe, the skin begins to feel hard and wooden. At that point, the victim needs to get to a doctor as soon as possible.

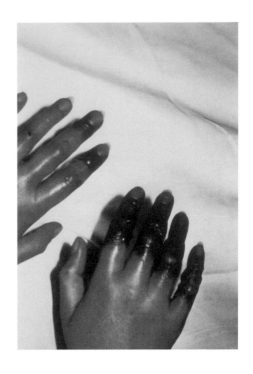

When the body loses more heat than it can produce, hypothermia results. Early indications of the condition include shivering, confusion and slurred speech, but victims will often insist that they are fine and do not require help. Quick action must be taken by others in the party to prevent further heat loss. Failure to do so may result in death within an hour.

Severe frostbite can result in the need for amputations.

Avalanches, as I have already mentioned, are the biggest snow hazard in the mountains, and affect the largest number of people. Just before I took on the job of alpine specialist, there were a number of unfortunate avalanche accidents in BC, including one on the highway near Terrace, another involving a mining company near Stewart, where sixty-eight people were caught in a slide that resulted in twenty-six fatalities, and four skier fatalities

at Whistler Mountain near Vancouver. It was obvious that comprehensive plans needed to be quickly established for several different user groups, and because we were some of the few who had knowledge and experience in this area, we soon had our hands full. It was important that the plans for each group or zone address not only the forecasting of avalanches (involving daily readings, snow pack profiles, weather analysis, among others), but also awareness (education, signs), prevention (closures, defense structures, etc.), and stabilization (control using avalanche guns).

The main groups that needed assistance in avalanche safety were highways, ski areas, helicopter and snowcat skiing operations, railways, mining companies, and backcountry enthusiasts.

At the time, forty-one public roads in BC and Alberta were affected by avalanches. In the late twentieth century, winter traffic volume on these roads was up to an average of 4,000 vehicles per day. As a result, highway closures due to high avalanche hazard had a considerable impact on commercial and private traffic.

Snow metamorphosis: the snowpack is a living thing.

Also at that time in Western Canada, six ski areas had major avalanche problems and carried out extensive avalanche control programs. These included some of the largest ski areas like Whistler and Lake Louise. An additional six others had moderate avalanche hazard levels that required continuous monitoring of snow conditions and occasional control. Finally in another seven alpine ski areas, avalanche hazard was considered minor.

Helicopter and snowcat skiing operates in potential avalanche terrain. Consequently, the forecasting of avalanche hazard is vital to the safety of skiers and success of the operators. In the 1980s, there were twelve heli-ski operations and three snowcat operations in existence. This represented approximately 35,000 skier days in a season.

Controlling the highway.

ABOVE Tony
Klettl loading
an Avalauncher
before the barrel
is attached.

FACING

Shot. Impact.

The three major railways in Western Canada—CP Rail, CN Rail and BC Rail—operated lines through a total of eight avalanche zones. Avalanches often interrupted the movement of trains and resulted in delays in the delivery of commodities and impacted the safety of crews.

In the 1980s, six mines were in operation in mountainous terrain. The principal avalanche problems were found on access roads to the mines.

Other industries also had to be careful. Hazards needed to be evaluated and predicted for crews using roads to relay stations on mountaintops, crews maintaining power lines and within forestry operations.

With the growth in backcountry users such as skiers, mountain climbers and snowmobilers, sound information on snowpack stability and avalanche hazard evaluation was essential. In my career, I felt that prevention was the most important area to focus on and that eighty-five to ninety percent of our time should go into preventative measures. There isn't much glory in prevention though—you can't prove how many people you saved by warning or educating them.

In response to the growing demand for avalanche safety all across the board, we set up study plots and carefully analyzed the weather. When all of the gathered information indicated that an avalanche was forming, explosives were the best way to settle the snow or trigger slides in a controlled situation before the hazard to the public became larger.

A few years before I returned to Jasper, the Icefields Parkway was opened and around the same time, Marmot Basin ski resort was first developed. Tony Klettl was put in charge of avalanche control in both areas. When I arrived, I could see that the equipment that he was using was not up to date. Tony and his team would walk up to the peak of the mountain with a rucksack full of dynamite and throw the charges in from above the slope, a two-day job. Often these ridges had large overhanging cornices. Although I didn't have much money to spend, I managed to get the needed equipment from different places. Then we ran people through training, took study plot data and weather readings, and charted the results.

Some time afterwards, I brought in the Avalauncher Mark 16, which was a compressed air gun. Actually, the Avalauncher started off as a baseball pitching machine, but years earlier in the US had been adapted for short-range avalanche control at ski areas. It could project a two-pound load of dynamite over a maximum distance of 2,000 metres using compressed nitrogen as a propellant. At the time, it was not very safe, but we played with it to make it as safe as possible. It evolved into a good avalanche control weapon.

Later, a group of us from different national parks tried to come up with a consistent plan for the use of avalanche control weapons for ski areas within the parks, like Sunshine and Marmot, and some outside the parks, like Panorama in Invermere, BC, as well as for highways. We travelled to Jackson Hole in the United States to observe what they did there.

Fred Schleiss, Peter Fuhrmann and I had very different ideas of what we wanted in the way of weapons. In Rogers Pass, they were using a Howitzer, which required a platoon of soldiers to operate and involved some terrific amounts of money. Fred wanted to continue with this system. Peter Fuhrmann pressed for controlling avalanches by dropping charges out of a helicopter. I, on the other hand, preferred a third type of guns, the Recoilers (the 75 and the 105). The Recoiler rifles were infantry weapons, which by then the army considered surplus equipment. This meant that unlike the Howitzer, we, the avalanche control team, could legally load and fire them rather than engaging soldiers to do so. The weapons were effective in doing what we wanted, which was to get the projectile into the trigger zone of the avalanche. It could be used in any weather, at any time of day, and it was the cheapest and most straightforward method — just push the stuff into the pipe at one end and blow it out the other. Ammunition for the Recoilers cost as little as six dollars at the time, while for the Howitzers it cost as much as $800. The Recoilers were safer too. I always felt that a helicopter and dynamite were not a great combination, and limited avalanche control to fair-weather days. In the end, we went primarily with the Recoilers, but Rogers Pass, with its huge control system in place, continued with the use of the Howitzers.

Approximately one out of every two people caught in an avalanche does not survive. Keep in mind, an avalanche can take three minutes to reach the valley floor; that's covering the same distance it takes a skier three hours to climb up.

When someone is caught in an avalanche and buried, speed is of the essence because the most common cause of death is suffocation. *If* the person was wearing an avalanche beacon (a Pieps or Skadi in those days), then his location in the slide could usually be determined within six minutes or less. Then the person had to be dug out.

People planning to travel into avalanche terrain for the first time usually take the time to learn and practice how to locate a person using an avalanche beacon. They rarely give much thought to shovelling however, thinking any idiot knows how to shovel. Yet shovelling appropriately may be the difference between life and death. Standing directly above the victim and digging straight down compacts the snow, and once the hole gets deeper, gives the shoveller very little room in which to maneuver or to efficiently move the snow away. Instead it is best to position oneself slightly down the slope and dig in a terraced fashion.

During my time in the avalanche business, we played around with several ideas on how to get oxygen down to the victims as quickly as possible, prior to shovelling. Ideas included a hollow probe stick through which air could be forced (foreseeable problems with this included snow blocking the tube as it was pushed down to the victim, and not knowing the victim's position in the snow in order to get the tube close to his or her mouth); a vest that would inflate with air as soon as it was impacted in some way such as by an avalanche (again, unless the person had a breathing tube to his mouth, this wouldn't be much help and the air certainly wouldn't last long anyway); or some way of establishing a large air space around the person's head within the slide (but how to do this?). Variations of these ideas are still being tossed around with some promising results.

In order to train wardens on how to safely travel through avalanche terrain, we needed some good routes for ski touring and snow travel training, preferably with great downhill slopes for carving a few turns. In Jasper, there are a lot of long valleys where you can walk up the hill on one side and then walk down

the other, because there is just not enough of a slope to ski down. Then we found the Eight Pass Route and it really filled the bill. As my imaginative name for it suggests, on a three-day trip, the route goes over eight passes, with a wide variety of winter travel conditions and some good steep slopes to ski down.

The scenery was something to behold, too, making one forget about the cold nights, blisters and heavy pack. The route leads up Hardisty Creek and then follows the north side of Mount Hardisty, Mount Kerkeslin and the Endless Chain Massive to Maligne Pass, and then down to Poboktan Creek. The total elevation gain is 3,100 vertical metres and the drop is over 2,600 vertical metres.

I used the Eight Pass Route for intermediate winter travelling training courses. The wardens learned to plan and prepare

The Eight
Pass Route.

for a trip, the ability to spot hazards along the route, winter travel techniques, safe crossing of avalanche slopes, route finding, and how to be prepared for emergencies, among other things. As well, they learned how to make and sleep in snow caves. It was an exceptionally good training ground.

Sometimes I took non-warden groups on ski touring trips to train as well. The RCMP, particularly those with search dogs, wanted to learn about avalanches and winter travel. We set up some schools, which I believe continue to this day.

In those early days, some funny things happened during those schools with the RCMP. At the time, most of the policemen were not very good skiers. I would have a number of guys and their dogs with me on a trip. If a guy fell, the dog would not accept him as his master any more. No matter what the officer said, the dog would run off and begin to fight with one of the other dogs. Sometimes we were on a steep side hill and there were five dogs and five masters all in one bundle in the snow, skis and poles lying everywhere.

Our training paid off when we were called to many winter rescues. There were several success stories, but also some really sad ones.

Mount Cleveland is in Glacier National Park in Montana, just across the border from Waterton National Park in Canada. The only access to the park was via Waterton Lake. We were called down to take part in a rescue there on the first of January one year. Four guys had planned to climb the north face of Mount Cleveland and they hadn't returned. Peter Fuhrmann drove down with three wardens from Banff and me with three wardens from Jasper. The lake was still not frozen, so the Waterton wardens ferried us across with all the equipment.

The US ranger in charge of the operation was a guy who had just completed one of my schools a week before and was a little antsy when I arrived.

Fuhrmann immediately went out to the site and found the climbers' camp. There was still a fire smoldering and some climbing equipment lying around, but no guys.

When I arrived, I suggested that a helicopter be brought in and that we begin to search that way. It took them a while to track down a helicopter, but finally a JB4 arrived with a pilot who had never flown in the mountains before. He was a total flatland flier and he really scared me. He had no idea about up- and downdrafts, and just flew straight into them. I flew around with him for a while, but eventually I said, "Let's go down and let somebody else have a go at this." Peter Fuhrmann went up with him for a while. They decided to go across the lake to refuel and just as they were about to land, the pilot said, "I'm passing out."

He fainted, resulting in a very hard landing that put the helicopter completely out of commission. The next day the US Air Force came with a great big machine. When we flew around we saw nothing on the north face but noticed a big avalanche on the west side and some stuff lying on the surface. We skied into the site and found a rucksack and a jacket lying on top of a large avalanche deposit.

This was before we had any dogs and the climbers weren't wearing beacons, so we had to form a probe line. At the bottom of the face was a large cliff with a big snow deposit above it and an even bigger deposit on the shallow slope below. A line of rescuers spaced about seventy-five centimetres apart (centre of the body to centre of the body) was formed across the lower avalanche deposit, everyone facing up the slope. Over three metre-long probes (one centimetre thick rigid steel tubing) were inserted deep into the snow in unison. If nothing feeling like a body under the snow was detected, the whole line pulled up their probes, moved half a metre forward and repeated the process.

At that point, it had already been almost a week since the climbers had gone missing, and the story had become big news in the American press. The news hounds were all over the place, including in Waterton trying to get information. They were not allowed to cross the lake with boats so they started flying around above us. I said that the noise of those planes might knock another avalanche loose and down on us, so in an act of extreme overkill, the US government established a huge no-fly zone over the rescue site. Even the airliners had to detour around us.

We had about twenty-nine or thirty people on the probe line, including some very well-known American climbers who were related to or friends of the missing. Meanwhile, the avalanche hazard was building again on the mountain slope above us. We didn't find anyone that day, so in the late evening I decided that we would set up the probe line once more the following day. When we were back out on the avalanche deposit the next day, one of the well-known climbers (all of whom were friends of mine) said, "How do you justify this? Thirty men under a slide like this, where there is obviously still some snow hanging above."

I said, "Avalanches don't fall out of the blue sky. They need a change, either in temperature, in precipitation or in wind."

The guys kept looking up as we probed and then one commented that the wind was coming up. Above, you could see the wind starting to drift the snow in. I looked at my watch and said,

"Well, in half an hour we're going to pull out."

Twenty minutes later somebody screamed, "Avalanche!!"

We all ran for it and a big duster came down. It dusted right over us, but there was no real danger, just a big cloud of powder. After that, we pulled out. Later that evening, I asked the pilot if he would fly me around once more, and there I saw a gigantic new avalanche deposit that had run over top the place where we had been probing hours earlier. Thankfully, we pulled out when we did.

We found the four guys in mid-summer in a canyon, still all roped together. Judging by where they were, approximately thirty to fifty metres of snow would have been piled on top of them following the accident. I don't know exactly how they got buried so deep. That remained a mystery to me.

A probe line at Mount Cleveland.

Another tragic rescue I will always remember taught me something about extreme persistence and the will to survive. There were four guys from Edmonton who came to climb a mountain in Jasper National Park in the wintertime. They were strong, experienced climbers who many of us knew. On the first day, they skied up the long approach route and then up the first buttress of the mountain to where they made camp.

One guy was cooking while another made snow caves. Most likely they weakened a cornice as they were digging and it collapsed, taking all four of them down with it. They ended up at the bottom of the climb. One guy, luckily, was lying on top of the snow. He checked himself out and found he had a broken arm, so he quickly supported it and then looked around for his friends. Another guy was lying on top but was very busted up. The final two guys were buried deep under the snow and he couldn't find them.

The injured guy, "Joe" (not his real name), was conscious and the first guy was able to speak with him. There were some sleeping bags lying around, so he collected them and bundled Joe up. Then he said, "Okay, I am going for help."

He went down that steep slope to the moraine where they had left their skis after the trip up the access path. Since he was not a confident skier, he decided not to take his skis and instead started hoofing it down in the knee-deep snow. By that time it was dark already, *plus* you may remember, he had a broken arm.

The going was not very easy, but he was determined. At what must have been about midnight, he came to a sharp curve where two paths led off in different directions. He mistakenly took the fork leading off to the left and after some time, came to a creek. The ice covering the creek was quite thin and when he stepped on it, he broke through. His feet now soaked in the sub-zero temperature, he crawled out of there and just kept going. After a kilometre or two, he realized he was going in the wrong direction and turned back.

When he finally got back up to the main path, feet freezing by that point, he walked another thirteen kilometres down to the highway through continuous deep snow. I am quite sure the only thing that kept him going was pure willpower and the resolve to help his friend.

He arrived at the highway in the afternoon of the following day where he flagged down a car. It turned out to be the wife of one of the wardens and she immediately phoned for help. The police came and picked him up.

It was a Sunday and I was skiing at Marmot Basin with my family. Once I was alerted of the accident, I quickly drove down to speak with the guy. He was sitting in the police car and despite his extreme effort to find help, was still quite awake and alert. He kept saying over and over, "Go and help my friend. Go and find Joe. You need to help Joe."

He gave me a very clear, precise description of where his friend was. We ordered the helicopter from Hinton and I sent a couple of guys up with skidoos. I flew up and from the helicopter could clearly saw the injured guy lying on top of the deposit in exactly the place his friend has described. We landed the machine on the deposit near him. When we checked, he was dead.

As soon as Alfie and Ginger arrived, we began the search for the other two guys. This was one of Ginger's first times in a real rescue situation. Due to conflicting scents from the not-yet frozen body in the sleeping bag and contamination from the helicopter as a result of landing in the search field, it took quite a while for

Ginger to find them. From that experience, we learned to make every effort not to land the helicopter in the area of the search during future rescues.

What I found amazing about this rescue was that if Joe had not been alive and had not talked to his friend following the slide, that guy would not have survived either. Trying to save Joe kept the friend going, so Joe's last act saved his friend's life.

Snowmobiling in the mountains was becoming more and more popular during that time, but the level of knowledge about avalanches among snowmobilers was very low. In the early eighties, a guy was caught in an avalanche in the area of Valemount, BC. Luckily, his friends saw exactly where he was buried and they dug him out alive. Following that accident, we kept suggesting to the snowmobile club in Valemount that they arrange for some education on avalanches and rescue methods. So eventually, they did. Gerry Israelson and I went to Valemount to teach two weekend courses about snow, avalanche awareness and rescue procedures.

One weekend following the completion of these courses, there was an accident at Clemina Creek, south of Valemount. Another group of snowmobilers from Alberta had parked right in the middle of an avalanche path halfway up the slope to eat lunch. Suddenly, the whole mountainside let go and a huge avalanche came down. Eleven people and ten skidoos were in its path. Five people were able to escape to the side, one was hit and injured but on the surface, and one dug himself out. The remaining four were under the snow. No one was wearing an avalanche beacon.

Some of the people who had completed our course the week before were also in the area and used the knowledge they had gained to start a rescue attempt. They helped uncover the one guy trying to dig himself out who was down near the bottom of the slide, and then they started to look around, trying hard to visually observe for anybody else.

One person on the sidelines immediately jumped on his snowmobile and went out for help. A policeman on duty in Valemount that day, who had also attended the avalanche school, was immediately in touch with the nearby helicopter-skiing operations. CMH, the closest, arrived first with a load of guides, followed by a team from Mike Wiegele Helicopter Skiing. They began searching with probes.

We had to come all the way from Jasper, so we were the last ones to arrive. Pretty soon the Weigele guys found one person, the CMH guys found another and an RCMP dog on the scene found another. All three had died.

At that point, one woman was still missing, but we had to call the search off due to nightfall and incoming bad weather. The wind howled all night and it was snowing hard. By the next morning, the hazard was so high that we didn't dare to go to the site of the accident. In order to make the search safer we used explosives to knock down the remaining snow on the mountain. We triggered another avalanche to run down overtop of everything. As a result, the site was safer but the scent of the buried person was gone for the search dog. He roamed around a little bit but couldn't indicate much.

We found the woman by probing. The snow was so deep that we used four-metre probes rather than the normal two-metre ones. By that time, it had been more than twenty hours since the accident, so the snow had settled and hardened. The stiffer probes would not penetrate the snow anymore; we had to switch to the soft probes. They were so flexible that they wouldn't go straight down into the snow, especially for the distance of four metres.

Finally, we located her and dug her out. She, of course, had not survived. It was a very tragic rescue, for everyone involved. The snowmobilers were all related and for the most part, completely unaware of the avalanche danger.

An inquest followed the accident and there were all kinds of ideas that came forward. Some people suggested that an avalanche bulletin that indicated whether the avalanche hazard in the Clemina Valley was high, moderate or low should be published every morning. I totally disagreed with this idea because there was not enough information to address this properly. A person sitting in Valemount wouldn't know what was going in Clemina. How had the temperatures, wind and precipitation affected the snowpack the night before? A forecast would just be a hell of a guess.

I told them about a similar plan that had been carried out in the neighbouring town to mine in Austria years before. The entire valley was a giant ski area with some avalanche problems. The innkeepers, guides and ski instructors all gathered together and formed a sort of avalanche-forecasting group. They put out a daily bulletin.

As it happened, a large avalanche came down across a road on one of the days the forecasting group had declared the avalanche hazard to be moderate. It knocked a bus full of Swedish skiers right off the road and into a canyon, covering the bus with many metres of snow. Thirty-two people drowned underneath all that snow, as the creek-water in the bottom of the canyon backed up. The victims were Swedish skiers, but the trip was organized by a German travel agency — and this agency decided to sue. They won the case and those poor bastards, the ski instructors and guides, who had made the prediction, had their wages garnisheed for years to come. I told the inquest to definitely not make that recommendation.

The main recommendation that resulted from the inquest was that avalanche slopes should be flagged so that people were aware of the serious terrain they were entering, and could make better decisions about where to snowmobile. They set up designated areas in the valley where people could stop to eat their lunch or fix their machines out of avalanche danger.

The next recommendation was to have regular courses available at the various snowmobile organizations to educate people about avalanche hazards. Snowmobilers would be taught to use avalanche beacons and how to be prepared by carrying proper equipment, like shovels, while sledding. All of these things pretty well happened.

Another interesting point that came of the inquest was that the deceased were all wearing helmets, and that the helmets became packed solid with snow between their faces and the helmet. The helmets had moved forward onto their noses and all four of the victims died of suffocation, mainly from the snow that was between the face and the helmet. Of course, buried in the deep snow, they could not get their hands up to do anything about this. We recommended that the helmet manufacturers have a look at the problem, which resulted in much better helmets becoming available — ones which do not move forward and are covered with face shields so the snow doesn't get inside.

Ski touring, powder skiing, winter climbing and snowmobiling are some of the great joys in life. But many times the line between delirium and disaster is very thin. Our job became helping that line become thicker through snow safety education.

Athabasca Glacier
in the 1960s.

7

THE SIDEHILLGOUGER SAYS,

"Travelling on the glacier is like bringing up your children.
Everybody thinks they can do it better, but no one knows
how it will turn out."

AS A GLACIER CREEPS SLOWLY DOWNHILL, it grinds and pushes almost everything out of its way with its massive weight, but even this enormous force has to yield to yet a more stupendous one — the mountain itself, the solid rock. These great creeping ice masses have to follow the contours of the rock below them, so a sudden drop or turn will put a terrific strain on the outer curve of the mass. Like in any case, if the elasticity of the material is over-strained, it will break. In a glacier's case, this provides the traveller with the thrill of "crevasses."

As the glacier moves down the mountain like a slow flowing river, these giant cracks (crevasses) in the ice open, close and change with the terrain. The slowness of its movement is demonstrated by the curious story of Ms. Julia O. On April 22, 1965, eleven members of the Canadian Alpine Club travelled up the Athabasca Glacier, unroped, above the first icefall in a heavily crevassed area. Ms. Julia O., travelling fourth in line, broke through a snow bridge and fell into the hidden crevasse below. She dropped about thirty metres and came to rest at the spot where the crevasse narrowed to approximately thirty centimetres. Below this spot the crevasse widened again and was another thirty-five metres deep.

Ms. O. was seriously injured by her fall, but due to a series of very fortunate circumstances, she was rescued and in hospital in record time, thus saving her life.

During the rescue, her skis, poles and rucksack were dropped into the void below her. Remember, this was April, 1965. On August 9, 1976, someone reported that he had found some equipment on the glacier. The wardens went up and found encased in ice Julia O.'s rucksack, skis and one pole. This equipment had travelled approximately one kilometre in eleven years. The skis were bent, but her lunch still looked edible.

If the previous winter's snow has melted or the wind has blown it away, crevasses are "open," or just half covered. It is perfectly safe to walk to the edge of an open crevasse providing you are standing on solid ice. A person who falls into one of these crevasses needs some smartening-up pills.

However, early in the season or higher up the glacier, crevasses are covered with snow and are hidden to the untrained eye. A knowledgeable person can find most of the hidden traps by looking out for the total crevasse system (depressions in the snow, changes of colour in snow or light reflections), or one can probe ahead with an ice axe or ski pole. It is impractical to probe for ten kilometres though, moving a metre forward at a time, so a combination of both methods (observation and probing) is necessary. There isn't a person alive, however, who can avoid all hidden pitfalls, either on a glacier or in life.

To back up our possible shortcomings, we must take preventative measures and therefore, travelling on a glacier requires a rope and teamwork. The ideal team is three people roped together, one behind the other, walking with the rope fully strung out. The general idea is, if one should misjudge the terrain, break through a snow bridge and disappear into the void below, the other two arrest the person's fall and pull him or her

A crevasse.

back to the surface, providing the team has taken all necessary precautions and has knowledge of crevasse rescue. If everything is done right, the chances of getting hurt are minimal, but one mistake can throw everything off and can result in the worst of consequences.

Thus, regular crevasse training sessions for the wardens were crucial. We often spent a week at a time out on the Columbia Icefields, or some of the other icefields and glaciers in the Rockies, practicing the various aspects of glacier travel. These included route-finding through heavily crevassed areas, building and living in igloos and snow caves, skiing roped up, and various phases of crevasse rescue.

These glacier trips made rescues easier because the wardens had already been in most of the places where rescues took place and they were familiar with the terrain. That saved our bacon more than a few times. I also felt that the wardens were the keepers of these vast pieces of real estate and should know what they had available to them. So I gave them the opportunity.

Team building was a vital part of rescue training and glacier trips were great for this. In the world we live in now, people rarely depend on someone else for their lives, but on the glacier or when climbing, you are committed to each other.

Over time we put a camp into every one of the icefields in the Rocky Mountain parks and climbed most of the surrounding peaks. Once, we started on the Columbia Icefields, travelled across numerous remote glaciers and ended up in Golden, BC — at the Mad Trapper Pub to be exact. We moved fast and managed to complete the trip in four days, climbing Mount Clemenceau in the process.

Due to their sheer size, one of the easiest ways to get into trouble on an icefields is to get caught in a whiteout. When the weather moves in, it can be difficult to tell the difference between the ground and the sky right in front of you. In typical white man's fashion, people often want to keep on moving despite conditions, finally ending up in a most undesirable place, if not already involved in an accident. The safest solution is to make camp and wait out the storm. If this is not possible, the key to avoiding an accident scenario is again preparation. Our teams carried and used thirty- to sixty-centimetre long bamboo wands with little flags affixed to one end. We placed one of these in the snow every second rope length across the icefields, then followed them safely

Nearing the peak of Mount Clemenceau.

The Columbia Icefields are 325 square kilometres in size and feed eight major glaciers. Beneath this thin layer of snow, the ice reaches depths of up to 365 metres.

back home, storm or no storm. These wands don't cost or weigh much. Naturally, in order not to litter or to lead others astray, all wands had to be removed on the return trip.

Once, on the Columbia Icefields, while conducting a school with the wardens, we had climbed the South Twin and then wanted to climb Mount Columbia. In order to do this, we needed to cross part of the Icefields again and move down into what is known as the trench, a dip or valley-like place in the field of ice. As we did this, the fog rolled in and stayed put for two days. It so totally socked us in that there was nothing we could do except make camp and wait it out. Wands did not help us in this situation because we were headed in a new direction, not backtracking.

Whiteout conditions
moving in.

On the third morning I gave up on the idea of climbing the mountain and said, "Okay, this is no good. Today we are going to go home via the Saskatchewan Glacier." We had come in via the Athabasca but we would go out via the Saskatchewan. "Abe, you lead us off."

So Abe looked at the compass and off he went. There were fifteen guys in all, on five ropes, three to a rope. I was the last one out of camp and as I stood there, the guys disappeared into the fog one after the other. Suddenly something caught my eye on my right side. I looked over and there was Abe coming straight at me. In the distance of a couple of kilometres at most, in the dense whiteout, he made a complete circle. I made it a little easier on him by saying, "Oh, you forgot something."

In planning for these trips, I would often buy the food for everybody and then we divided it up to carry. The health fanatics in the group, particularly those going out on their first longer trip, would look at all the sugar and bacon I bought with disgust. I would say, "Okay, if you don't like it, leave it here."

So a lot of them would leave the sugar and the bacon behind, instead throwing in some vegetables and energy bars.

On the first day out they would see me frying up some bread in the bacon grease left over from my dinner, and snicker. By the second day the disgust had gone away and by the third they had a look of longing. Some would ask me if they could lick the pan after I was done. The same would go for the sugar. By the third day my sugar was gone, because everybody kept coming to borrow some for his or her tea. With the miles we put on in the cold, you just needed that grease and sugar, no matter what you believed about healthy food.

Sometimes, on days that we had a long, boring distance to cover, we would start up silly conversations to distract us. Everyone would get involved. One time, for example, we discussed all the possible theme songs for our line of work. Another time we explored all of the possible uses of pancakes — a hat, a Frisbee, a chest warmer, to name just a few.

Once we were caught in a storm and we had to hole up in our tents for four days, the wind howling the whole time. When we finally emerged, the teams were frustrated and bored with all that inactivity. I needed to say something to make them feel better, so I told them, "The most important thing right now is that we should try and keep our bodies clean while we are up here doing this stuff. For heaven's sake, we should at least all change our underwear! So … you guys in this tent here, you change with those guys over there and this tent, you change with the other team there…." No one followed my advice.

When we were caught in storms like that, I gained the reputation for having an extremely large bladder. I would drink gallons of tea and have a large bowl of noodle soup for dinner, both of which we cooked in our tents as we waited out the storm. The other guys would then have to climb out of their nice warm sleeping bags and into the raging blizzard to take a piss. I never seemed to have to and they would all wonder at my amazing ability to hold it. I, of course, told them it was due to my superior Austrian genes, but actually, I had a secret — in the form of an L-shaped slit cut into the floor of my tent.

Since anything that went through that hole sunk into the snow and almost immediately froze, my tent modification worked really well. One time though, we were out on a trip, and that first evening I drank a lot of tea before going to sleep. By the middle of the night, I really needed to go, so I started feeling all around the floor of my tent. Where was the hole? After searching for quite a while, I had to give up and go outside.

The next day, I found out that about a week before our trip, Gerry Israelson's wife, Leslie, had been in what we called the rescue room, the place where we stored all of our gear when not using it. While there, she noticed that there was a hole in the bottom of my tent. "Oh, poor Willi," she thought to herself. "I'll just have to take this home and sew it up for him."

We were involved in numerous glacier rescues — some lucky, some funny, some very dangerous, and too many of them tragic. More dumb things have been done by people on glaciers than in all other mountaineering activities combined.

Sometimes a successful rescue was just a matter of someone being alert. At the toe of the Athabasca Glacier there are always tourists walking, running and climbing on the glacier and as a result, somebody is always falling into one of the small terminal crevasses. One day, a warden named Johnny Wackerle came walking down from the glacier at the end of the day. We had just completed a training school and he was the last one down. There was new snow on the glacier and he noticed a fresh set of footprints going over to one of the crevasses that had caused trouble in the past, but no track coming back. Being a guide, he was alert to the situation. He couldn't see anybody around, so he walked over and looked into the crevasse. Sure enough, there was a guy down in there, a tourist travelling alone, who had wandered out onto the glacier, unaware of the dangers. He had fallen into the crevasse and was unable to get out. If Wackerle had not been so alert, that guy would have probably spent the night down there and been in serious trouble.

Another time, a little dog belonging to Jasperite Barb Pugh fell into a crevasse near the toe of Athabasca Glacier. Somebody would have to go down into the crevasse and get that dog out of there.

The dog was approximately fifteen metres down and was wedged into the ice where the crevasse narrowed. Because he was quite small, he had fallen further into the narrows than a human would have. The dog howled terribly and a lot of people had gathered around by the time the wardens arrived. There was no lack of advice on how to proceed.

Somebody had to go down into the crevasse and get that dog out of there.

Hans Fuhrer, a small, wiry warden, was selected for the job. We roped Hans up and lowered him into the crevasse, but the dog was so far down in the narrow section that he couldn't reach him. We had to pull Hans back up and try a new approach. This time we tied the rope to Hans's ankles and down he went, head first.

Being in a crevasse is not a very secure feeling at the best of times; they are created by the movement of glacial ice after all. A crevasse can suddenly close just as easily as it can open.

Being lowered headfirst was definitely a strange sensation for Hans. He wiggled himself into the narrows and grasped hold of the unfortunate dog. Upon returning to the surface, Hans, with his Swiss accent, said, "If this crevasse would have closed on me, you could have sent me home in an envelope."

Another rescue began when a warden stationed at the Icefields spotted two people and a dog walking side by side through the first icefall on the Athabasca Glacier, an area of many crevasses. They had no rope, no rucksack and were wearing inappropriate clothing, in the late afternoon on a wintry day.

By eight p.m. the warden reported that they were still not back. The temperature went below −5°C and a storm was moving down from the Icefields above. Tony Klettl, Jim White and I took White's snowmobile and headed up the moraine to see if we could spot them. Sure enough, there they were quite a distance up the glacier. It was easy to see them because one guy was wearing what looked like bright white pants.

Assuming that they would not survive such a night, we started off in the pitch black at nine p.m. and followed their footprints through the mess of seracs and crevasses of the lower icefall. By midnight we caught up to them.

Their dog was howling due to frozen feet. They reported that three times they had fallen into crevasses, but luckily had been able to extract themselves. During one of those falls, one of the guys had landed in a puddle of water and gotten his blue jeans soaking wet. He decided to remove them, thinking they would dry out. Without his body heat, the pants almost immediately froze solid, so he wasn't able to get them back on. For that reason, there he was, standing in front of us in his very white "Stanfield Specials." This explained why we had been able to see him so clearly from a distance.

Luckily, 'underpants guy' didn't yet have frostbite on his legs. We gave him a pair of wind pants to put on. Then we tied the whole works, including their dog, onto our rope and started making our way down. A short distance along, a snow bridge broke behind me and I fell backwards down into a crevasse. Tony held me (with the rope) and got me back out.

Once off the glacier, we started up the snowmobile for the approximately five kilometre trip back to the parking lot. We followed the unplowed road that is used in the summer for taking tourists on snowcoach glacier tours. From the glacier, the road heads up onto the lateral moraine and then down to the toe of the glacier. A long scree slope that is part of the moraine falls off steeply from the left side of the road all the way down to the glacier. Near the highest point of that scree slope that night, there was a huge snowdrift across the road. Due to its height, it was impossible to go over it, so Jim White, driving the snowmobile and pulling a trailer behind, decided to get off of the machine to lead it around the snowdrift. There was very little space to maneuver, with the steep slope of the moraine falling off on his left, but since he had managed to do it successfully on the way to the glacier, he wasn't worried. He positioned himself on the lower (scree-slope) side of the machine.

All of a sudden when he was halfway across, the skidoo spun out and the whole thing started to slip down the slope. The snowmobile knocked Jim over and he went flipping down the steep moraine, ass over teakettle. The snowmobile and trailer were flipping down right there beside him, sparks flying in all directions. The snowmobile, the trailer and the warden were all heading the same way: down.

Meanwhile, at the top, underpants guy had witnessed Jim's fall. When there was no motion below, his conscience got the best of him, I guess. He said, "Oh my, oh my…" and then stepped out over the edge and copied Jim.

Down he went, ass over teakettle. Holy shit, now there were two guys lying down there! After the dust had settled for the second time, there was twice as little motion as before.

I ran down the road to try to get over to them and help. Then I heard the snowmobile engine start up. Jim came around and up the road again with the snowmobile, underpants guy sitting on the back. Luckily, neither of them broke any bones, but Jim was pretty banged up and sore. The accident laid him off work for almost three weeks.

When Jim got the snowmobile back up to the snowdrift, we set a belay with the climbing rope on the machine so it couldn't take off on us again. We made it across and got everybody home safely. Well, you can't win them all.

Any person who travels on a glacier will likely, sooner or later, end up several feet below the surface. To pull a fallen person back out of the hole takes, at times, considerable skill.

An ice bridge.

First of all, the fall has to be stopped, and then free rope is needed to set up a pulley or Bilgari rescue system. A three-person team always has free rope between the first and second anchorman. A two-person team has to either rope into one-third of the rope from each end and carry one-third to have it readily available, or they need to rope one person in the middle and the other at one end. Both ends must be attached to the second person, and great care must be taken to ensure that weight be only on a single strand while the other strand is readily available for rescue set-up.

A number of years ago, we hauled two men out of the Columbia Icefields. They represented a classic example of the double rope system. The men had registered out for a climb on Mount Columbia and were overdue. Poor weather did not permit us to fly, so we sent one party up the Athabasca Glacier and another party up the Saskatchewan in search of them. Travel was exceptionally bad. Eight times members of the rescue teams fell in crevasses, so it was an easy assumption that our "overdues" had crevasse problems. We found them that same night camped in a heavily crevassed area waiting for us. One man had a smashed kneecap and a few bruises on his head, and the other was okay.

What happened was this: The previous day they had travelled on a double rope through this area; the snow was wet and soft, the bridges weak. The first guy fell into one huge crevasse, bridge and all. By the time everything came to a standstill, he was thirty metres down and hanging free on the rope.

The second man was in a perfect arrest position, lying on his stomach, ice axe dug in, bodyweight overtop it, but only about two metres from the edge of the crevasse. It was not cold enough for the rope to freeze into the ice and the guy below was too far away from either wall of the crevasse to anchor himself to it somehow, so his entire weight was on the man above for the whole time.

The upper guy tried to get an ice screw off his belt and screw it into the ice as a way to take some of the weight off himself and to stabilize everything. When he had the screw halfway into the ice, he lost his traction slightly and slipped almost a metre toward the crevasse. He couldn't reach back to where the screw was while still holding the rope and the climber below, so he started the whole maneuver once more. He was screwing in another ice screw when a chunk of ice broke off under the ice axe. Once more, he started sliding toward the crevasse. Thirty eternal centimetres later, he stopped everything again. Now he was less than a metre from the edge of the open crevasse and the second screw was out of reach, too.

By that time his feet were sticking out over the edge of the crevasse so he knew that he had to do something drastic. With no relief in sight, he gingerly untied his chest harness and dropped the whole works. The guy below fell another fifteen metres to where the crevasse narrowed. He banged his head and

smashed one kneecap, but was still conscious. The fellow above then started to have second thoughts about his action, so he proceeded to collect all available string from the tent, packsack, windbreaker, shoelaces, etc. He tied them all together and lowered this line down to his partner. The partner tied the loose end of the climbing rope to the string and the guy above hauled it up. Then he rigged a pulley system and inch by inch he pulled his partner up. After five hours of continuous work, his partner was hoisted back up to the land of the living.

They then did the smartest thing they could do — they set up camp and waited for us. The only problem was they didn't realize that their tent was set up right on a snow bridge of yet another crevasse.

Luckily, the weather cleared a bit and I was able to fly in with the helicopter. I could see very clearly from above the precariousness of their camping spot. Snow on a bridge over an open crevasse is lighter in colour than snow with solid ice underneath it. We had to land quite a ways away in order not to knock the bridge down with the propeller wash.

I took all of the equipment I needed and went over as close to the two men as I could. Then I told the uninjured guy *not* to stand up, to just lie there because he and his partner were right over a crevasse. He told me that the other guy had head injuries and a shattered knee. I asked him to just tie his friend into the rope I had thrown over to them and I would pull him off the snow bridge and over to me, which I did.

Several times during this procedure, the first guy wanted to stand up so I repeatedly had to remind him to keep low. Once I had pulled his friend to safety, I wanted to pull him over as well.

Before doing so, the guy asked if he could gather up his tent and equipment, but I convinced him to forget about it.

One of many rescues.

Once I had pulled both men off of the snow bridge, we loaded them into the helicopter and as we did so, the team of wardens that had travelled all the way up the Saskatchewan Glacier on skis arrived. Both teams, we heard later, had had an exceptionally difficult time of it because of the rotten snow conditions. As the pilot and I lifted off with the rescued men, the snow bridge they had been camping on collapsed into the crevasse, tent and all. We flew the two guys out and then the pilot went back for the wardens.

One of the most emotionally difficult rescues I took part in during my career was that of Cliff Brown, a local Jasper boy. At the age of nineteen, he was not much older than my own kids. We got the call one evening that Cliff had fallen into a crevasse on Mount Athabasca and that he was still alive. His brother had stayed with him on the mountain while the others in the party went for help. Actually we found out later, Cliff had fallen in the crevasse in the act of saving his brother. Following the accident, the others were able to help the brother, but could not get Cliff out, so they descended the mountain for help.

By the time we took the call and were ready to go, it was too dark to fly. I put two teams together to climb up to the accident site. I remained at the bottom with the radio. They arrived onsite at midnight and immediately lowered a guy down to check on Cliff's condition. Word was sent up that he was still breathing. He was about fifty metres down and really jammed in, which made it very difficult to extract him. There was very little room to maneuver with the shear ice of the crevasse narrowing in on both sides. By that time, Cliff's body heat had warmed the ice around him and then had refrozen, making him very stuck.

The guys obviously didn't want to injure him further as they tried to free him from the ice, so progress was fairly slow. By six a.m., they had him out. At that time it was already light enough to use the helicopter, so I flew up to the rescue site, while the team carefully packed Cliff into the stretcher. The helicopter landed and we loaded him inside.

Amazingly, after such a long drop into the crevasse, several injuries and a very cold night, Cliff was still alive and semi-conscious. I sat with him in the helicopter and supported his head.

Actually, he was holding his own head up and grabbing onto my arm with quite a strong grip. In his semi-conscious state, he must have realized that his situation was changing, because about three minutes before landing, where a doctor and an ambulance were waiting for him, his grip loosened and his head fell back. As I sat there with him, I felt powerless, and could only keep repeating to him, "Not now, Cliffy, not now."

We made it down, got him into the ambulance and to the hospital. He remained unconscious for three months, but did survive. With the same determination that kept him alive in the crevasse, he fought his way back to independence and still works and lives in Jasper.

The Bugaboos.

8

THE SIDEHILLGOUGER SAYS,

"If you fall, fall slowly and enjoy the scenery on the way down. You may as well, because it's not the fall that will hurt you — just the sudden stop at the bottom."

IN ADDITION TO THE HIGH PEAKS, the Canadian Rockies are also known for their many beautiful canyons and waterfalls. No matter how often a person sees a natural phenomenon, such as Maligne Canyon or Takakkaw Falls, one remains in awe. Thus the easily accessible canyons and waterfalls situated in or near the main valleys of the parks attract many visitors.

In the off-season, a person can really enjoy a sightseeing trip to one of these places, but during tourist season, unless you want to grow an instant ulcer, it's best to keep away. Typically there are tourists on top of the fences built to keep them safe, beyond the fences and knee-deep in the water immediately above water-falls. Some people even attempt to climb on the canyon walls, while young kids run around playing and pushing each other, unaware of the dangers.

I once saw a fellow doing a handstand on the balustrade of the Athabasca Falls Bridge. Another time I saw a guy fording the turbulent waters immediately above the falls with his little girl on his shoulders. He was trying to make it to the centre rock. The mother of the girl was behind the fence on the north side, taking pictures of father and daughter's heroic, but not so smart, moves. When the water came up to his thighs he retreated. I tried to talk to him and he told me to mind my own business.

One time I was involved in a search for the body of a man who had fallen into a waterfall a few days earlier. The river was running high, but every so often we would go and check the backwaters out in the canyons below the falls to see if we could find him. Usually drowning victims disappear in the muddy, dirty water of summertime, making it very difficult to retrieve them.

While I was searching there, I saw a group of kids over the fence, playing near the edge of the waterfall. There was no water running near where they were, but there was a rock slab dampened by spray from below that slanted right down into the falls. These kids were pretending to push each other into the falls. One little guy, about six years old, tried to play with the older ones, but he couldn't quite keep up. So instead, he jumped down from a rock ledge onto the wet slab below. He slipped and landed on his behind, but by some miracle, stopped and didn't fall any farther.

I went over and called him up to ask him where his parents were. "Oh, I don't know. They're around, but my grandfather is over there."

I went over to this elderly gentleman and told him what had happened. "You should call your grandkids away from there," I said. "This is not a playground. Almost every year we fish a corpse or two out of these waters. In fact, that is exactly what I am doing now, looking for a man who fell in here a couple of days ago."

The old gentleman half smiled, patted me on the shoulder and replied, "I am quite sure they will fence off a little piece of Heaven for you when you die."

If he hadn't been so old, I would have plowed the guy one. He didn't call the kids.

Sometimes the tourists and/or the rescue teams really had luck on their side. One day for example, a man fell into Maligne Canyon and was washed down to just below the Fourth Bridge. He managed to hold onto a rock in the middle of the stream. I just happened to be driving nearby when the call came in, so I turned around and headed for the canyon. I had a rope and other equipment with me in the vehicle, which I grabbed. Numerous people were standing around watching the fellow below holding onto the smooth, slippery rock in the rushing water. He was already tired and somewhat hypothermic. Just below the rock he was clinging to was another small waterfall.

I knew he would not be able to hang on there much longer, and I also knew that a few wardens would arrive soon to help me out. So I put the rope around myself, tied the other end to a tree and lowered myself down. I reached where he was, grabbed him and pushed him onto a rock shelf nearby. Then I just waited for the wardens and when they showed up, they quickly pulled us out. The guy lived.

As it was with the earlier story about the dog in a crevasse, we didn't just rescue people. One time a very distressed lady came to the warden office, explaining that her Dachshund had fallen into the Maligne Canyon. He was on a rock shelf hollowed out in the wall of the canyon and was howling down there. We put a team together and went for a look-see. What had happened was that the dog chased a squirrel and had simply run out of ground beneath his feet. He went right over the edge of the canyon and landed thirty metres lower in a quiet pool of water between the Third and Fourth Bridge, where he was able to swim to a ledge under a large overhang. He was running back and forth on the ledge, crying for his master.

We had to set up for a complete rescue and lower a fellow down into the canyon. Luckily, the dog was not badly injured so the rescuer didn't have much trouble with him. Both of them were hoisted to the surface and "Waldy" was returned to his master. That was the only rescue ever that we did not have to write a report on.

Many times people (and dogs) weren't so lucky. Although almost all the canyon rims were fenced off by that time, most of the accidents occurred in these fenced areas. We were called out at least ten times a year because someone was down in the water. In many cases, we or someone else succeeded in getting them out alive, but the statistics were still grim. In 1969, seven people drowned in Jasper National Park alone.

Some of the accidents were really tragic, particularly when they involved children. I would often think of my own children during such times and count my blessings.

In trying to understand an accident, relatives and friends of the victims tended to look for reasons why it occurred or for someone to blame. My experiences in these situations, as well as during rescues in the mountains and on the glaciers, showed me that these answers could not always be found. Some people could take all the chances in the world and get away with it, while others only needed to make half a mistake or just have really bad luck and it was all over.

When someone fell into a river and we didn't manage to find him or her on the first day, a quick recovery became much harder. We had somewhat of a chance in a clear-running river, but in the silt-laden rivers that ran off from the glaciers, it was almost impossible. After the first day, a drowning victim's body will sink. Then between the ninth and eleventh day, it will bloat and rise. I would set some traps in the river below the spot where the person fell in. When the body came floating down, it would sometimes get hung up on those traps.

Sadly, some of the bodies were in the river for weeks. I remember finding one guy after a long search, caught up in some driftwood. The body was already in a state of decay, but amazingly after weeks in the water, the guy's Timex was still ticking.

If we couldn't find the body, Alfie and Ginger would look for it in the fall, when the river level was low.

Accidents happened in somewhat more remote places as well. One day we had a report that two teenagers had gone to Ogre Canyon, near the eastern boundary of Jasper National Park. They hadn't returned, so we went out to search for them.

We located their car and some of their belongings near the upper end of the canyon. So we began the search by entering the canyon at the top end and followed it down. After some distance, there was a drop-off of about fifteen metres, where we noticed a rope hanging down, which did not quite reach the bottom of the canyon wall. From what I saw, I made the assumption that the boys had rappelled down but were unable to get back up again because the end of the rope was then just out of reach from below. We continued down the canyon until a waterfall stopped us.

After returning the way we came and searching the canyon from the sides, we finally located both boys a distance apart from each other but near the base of the waterfall we had retreated from earlier. We set up a cable and lowered a warden wearing a full wet suit down through the waterfall to carry out the recovery. Tragically, neither of the boys survived.

I learned something important that day however. At one point during the search we decided to go down to the bottom end of the canyon and try to come up from below. There is a narrow dirt road running along the Athabasca River near the base of the canyon. Looking up from the road, we could see a second waterfall formed by water shooting out over the top of a big overhang, like the spout of a teapot, and landing in a rounded bowl-like basin. There was not a single crack in the completely smooth rock wall. The team and I stood at the bottom of this, deciding what to do.

"The walls are vertical and completely smooth. How in hell are we going to get up there?" I wondered aloud.

"It's so smooth we won't be able to get a piton in. There are no holes anywhere, no cracks, no nothing," another guy added.

"Jesus, we are going to have to drill our way up."

We kept talking back and forth like this, throwing out ideas on how best to approach the problem. Meanwhile, a policeman, standing with us, who knew nothing about mountaineering, listened to us for a while. Then he leaned over to me and said, "What about a ladder?"

That totally floored me. We normally worked in very remote places and were thinking like mountaineers, not construction workers. We had overlooked the obvious. That day reminded me again of the importance of listening to everyone, whether they were mountaineers or had some other field of expertise. Different perspectives were valuable.

Anyway, we went and got a ladder, stretched it out and within two minutes we were above that waterfall.

Most accidents in hiking and scrambling are caused when a person loses his footing. It can happen to anyone when, totally unexpectedly, a foot or both feet shoot out from underneath him and he ends up in a very undignified position. Then, depending on where this happens, be it a steep side hill or beside a rushing river, it can become more than just undignified.

The most important piece of equipment needed to gain reasonable footing in the mountains is a good pair of boots. They must give support to the ankles, protection for the feet and, most importantly, have a good sole.

Still, to avoid some of these nasty falls, a person must also know where the slippery places are. For instance, a windfall with the bark still on — step onto it, the bark peels off and it really takes you for a leap. Or grass on a steep side hill, dry or wet, and in particular, long and across the ground — never to be trusted. Beware of a scree slope that gets steep at the bottom and ends with a rock slab or large rocks. It's fun at first, to move down with the loose scree, but then the little rocks start to act like ball bearings underfoot. Everything moves in the same direction: downwards! And the slope steepens and the pace gets faster and it all leads right into the rock slabs below. The only way out is to run off to the side, if it's not already too late.

Wet rocks too, are usually slippery, depending on the kind of rock. If rocks are covered with lichen and it starts to rain, travelling can become treacherous.

Silt or glacier dust can also be a problem. When a silt-carrying river recedes, it leaves residual silt on the rocks, especially on rock slabs above waterfalls. This usually appears harmless because it's dry, but it can be as slippery as ice. Be warned.

Very early on, in each of the parks, we set up binders outlining climbing routes and providing information to prospective

ROCHE-A-PERDRIX 7002′

A For Routes 2, 3, 4, & 5 Park Car
At Rock Quarry (100 Yds East Off
Highway) Take Game Trails To Start
Of Climb

2 Gully Route (Apr Grade 3 *)

3 Chimney Route (Apr Grade 4

4 N W Ridge (Apr Grade 5

5 Easiest Descent Route
Equipment: Rock Climbing.

A For Route 1 Park Car Near Fiddle
River, Bushwalk To Start Of Climb
Equipment: Rock Climbing.

climbers. Each party interested in doing a climb was then required to sign out at a parks office, providing information about exactly who was in the party, what their planned route was, their start date and an expected return date. A party that was overdue (had not returned by the expected return date) alerted us of the need for a rescue. Other times we were told about an accident situation by climbers either from the affected party or from other parties climbing in the area.

A page from a climbing route binder.

Sling system.

One time, a climbing party came into the Banff warden office and reported that there was a dead guy lying up on Mount Cascade. The wardens asked the climbers a number of questions, and from the description of their reaction to the grisly find, the position of the body and the general location, the wardens concluded that the man may not be as dead as they assumed.

Speed was of the essence. The helicopter was called, rope and stretcher were rigged underneath, and Peter Fuhrmann, who was sporting a large beard at the time, was strapped into the heli-rescue seat. Once his radio helmet was on and he had attached himself to the O-ring at the end of the cable, away they went, Peter hanging twenty metres below the machine.

At the scene of the accident, Jim, the pilot, put Peter and the stretcher gently down on the ground. Peter unhooked and Jim, with the counter-weighted rope, flew away. Peter examined the patient. He was pale, quite rigid, had no visible injuries, but did have a faint pulse. Looking around for more clues, Peter quickly noticed several empty aspirin bottles lying on the ground near the guy. It became clear that the man was attempting suicide. He had climbed up the mountain a little ways to be closer to God and then overdosed on the aspirin pills.

There was not much first-aid that could be administered in a case like this, so Peter loaded him into the stretcher. Since the patient was quite stiff and unconscious, Peter didn't bother to tie him down very tightly. The helicopter was called back, Peter hooked himself and the stretcher onto the rope and away they flew.

In mid-air, a good thousand metres above the valley bottom, the guy started to stir. He opened his eyes and looked around.

His eyes focused and he stared at the bearded face above him. "Who are you?" he asked.

Peter answered in a deep booming voice, "I am Peter."

After a long pause, the man decided that maybe he wasn't ready to enter the pearly gates quite yet, so he tried to get out of the stretcher. Since he was not tied in very well, Peter had to use all his strength to hook a leg and his arms around the man, to prevent him from falling out. After struggling for a few minutes, Peter freed one hand to push the button on the radio. He hollered through the walkie-talkie, "Down, Jimmy, down! This guy is trying to get away!"

They made it down and to the hospital safely.

Peter and Jim returned to base with a smile and a story, "Guess what happened to me today on the way to the hospital?!"

Rescue on a rock face.

Another rescue began when some people called in and said that there were two guys halfway up a mountain face in Jasper Park, screaming for help. So we went to have a look with the helicopter and soon found them. As reported, they had climbed halfway up the face when it began to rain. The temperature dropped, the rain froze and the whole mountainside was soon covered in *verglas* (a thin layer of ice). The climbers couldn't move up or down for fear of slipping and thus had already been stuck up there for a day. The wind was blowing strongly, making the flying ferociously bad. Gary Forman, the pilot, and I both looked from inside the helicopter to where the men were stranded and thought, "Oh my God, what are we going to do now?"

The two guys were in a place where the rock face was almost completely vertical, which made it very difficult for the helicopter to get in close enough to reach them. We flew around a couple more times and then Gary said, "I think I know how we can make it in there."

So we flew to the base of the mountain to hook up the helicopter sling system. A number of wardens were standing there at the bottom. I explained what the situation was and then said, "Okay, who wants to go?"

They all started looking up at the clouds and the mountains and everywhere else but at me. "So, okay then, I'll go myself," I said.

I hooked my harness into the sling and we flew in. When we got close to where the men were, Gary maneuvered the helicopter in such a way that he caused me to swing slightly toward the rock face. I couldn't quite reach the cliff, so I held out my hand and one of the guys pulled me in. I quickly realized I shouldn't have done that because I had a recently dislocated shoulder and it was still healing. When the guy grabbed my arm and tried to pull me in, it almost dislocated again. But anyway, I made it. After I hooked into a piton fixed on the rock face and Gary flew away, I proceeded to put extra seat harnesses that I had with me, onto both of the guys. When we were ready, Gary swung the cable back to us, I quickly hooked one of the men onto it and Gary flew him out.

I then set everything up so that when Gary returned for the second guy, we could both get onto the cable and be transported off the mountain face. I realized I had to challenge my mettle here, to see how well I reacted under stress.

The thing was that I had a brand new pair of gloves that I had bought in Mexico. I put the gloves on a ledge. The guy and I were both tied to the rock, the wind was still blowing ferociously and I knew we wouldn't have much time once the helicopter arrived and Gary swung the sling back in. So in my head I had it all planned out. When the helicopter came, I would give one of the two rings at the end of the cable to the guy and I would take the other. We would both hook in, I would give the signal to Gary, I would pull the loop loose that tied us tight against the rock, I would grab my gloves and then off we would go.

Everything happened exactly the way I had it anticipated until I pulled loose from the rock face and the helicopter began to lift up. The guy had his hand over top his carabiner and I couldn't see if he was hooked in properly, so I reached over to pull his hand away. He wouldn't let go, so I had to yank it really hard. He was hooked in correctly, but by that time my gloves were about fifteen centimetres out of reach. And that's where they probably still are today, up on that face. Once again, you can't win them all.

When we flew out, I thought the wind was going to rip the clothing off my body, it was so strong. But we both got down without anybody coming to harm.

Most rescues went well, but every so often we had a really close call. As I said earlier, I learned to trust my intuition and it saved my life or the life of a warden on more than one occasion.

One of these close calls came right at the beginning stages when the whole rescue program was in its infancy. I was at Camp Coleman conducting a fall regional warden training for Walter Perren. We had an improvised rescue practice, using a metal stoke litter, which was like a mine rescue basket. It was the equipment we had at the time. We put Smoky Guttmann in. Then with one guy leading the litter, we used the ropes to lower this thing down. We came to a ledge under a vertical face and I said to ole Stenson, who was leading the litter, "Go over there. Put him over there so that he's out of the way of any rockfall."

So Stenson dragged the stretcher over, underneath a small rock overhang. I was the only one standing out on that ledge. One after the other, the guys above rappelled down. Everybody knocked a few small pebbles off, which was okay, but then the last guy knocked a rock off that was about as big as a fist. That rock came down through a little bit of a gulley. It bounced a few times back and forth between the gulley walls and then moving almost horizontally to the rock face, in one long jump it flew over and landed right above where the guys with the stretcher were standing.

It just so happened that while we had been standing there, it started to snow. Some really big, moist snowflakes came down.

Offhandedly, I said, "Why don't you take Smoky out of the stretcher before he gets soaking wet? We'll tie him back in again afterwards."

So they unhooked him and Smoky crawled out of the stretcher. In the instant that he crawled out of there, the fist-sized rock that had been bouncing down the gulley flew straight across, hit a more than twenty kilo rock just above the stretcher and knocked it off. That huge rock then fell down right into the middle of the now empty stretcher causing it to double right up. That damn thing would have hit Smoky right in the middle, too, and caused some major injuries. Stenson, the guy leading the stretcher, was still hooked onto the front of it. The twenty kilo rock broke into a thousand pieces and one piece hit Stenson on the wrist, breaking it (his wrist, not the rock). That was the only trouble we had on that one.

Another time we climbed Mount Kerkeslin on skis in the wintertime, travelling up a gulley. Near the top, Kerkeslin has a couple of vertical towers, below which are open areas on 30-degree slopes. We were not roped-up. When we were almost at the open areas at the bottom of the vertical towers, I stopped and looked around. It wasn't steep so I'm not sure why I stopped. Everybody else stopped next to me and all of a sudden—WHUMPF. We heard this big sound and immediately thought a cornice must have broken off one of the towers. Sure enough, it hit the slope in front of us and knocked that whole slope out of there in a giant avalanche. Where we stood, our skis were almost sticking out over the fracture line. We all just looked at each other and then one guy asked, "Why did you stop here?" and all I could say was, "I don't know."

The British Army brought soldiers over to the Canadian Rockies for many years to train. Well, with those guys there was always trouble. They would go climbing or into the back-country or on the rivers without consulting any map or asking for any information. The idea was to go some place where none of them had been before and nobody knew the way. They would always get three or four days behind schedule and be in some place altogether different from where they were supposed to be. When we rescued them and took them out by helicopter, they would get really mad.

Over the years, a couple of guys were killed. There was one mountain accident and another on a river. I was told by one of the officers that they were allowed to lose one percent of their crew each year. Out of a hundred guys, they could come home with one less without repercussions.

One time they were on a mountain, three days overdue. We had already looked for them the day before and they refused a rescue. They were coming off on the west face on a route that was too difficult, forcing them to retract again. So what we did was put a radio, which was turned on, a few chocolate bars and some water into a bag. Then we lowered it down to those guys and talked to them on the radio. We asked them to pick up the radio and answer us but they refused. They walked by it while the radio was talking away at them. How boneheaded.

Anyway, when they were several days overdue, I decided we were not going to fool around with this situation any longer and needed to get these guys off of that mountain right away. The longer we left them up there, the more likely it was that they would make a stupid risky decision, leaving us to clean up the mess. So the helicopter flew up and found a place to land, and then we told the soldiers to get into the helicopter or else we'd have to sling them off. Gerry Israelson flew up and hooked two guys up. One of the guys had put his ice axe in the flap of his rucksack so the shaft stuck out horizontally, rather than strap it in the back vertically like everyone else did. The helicopter lifted off and luckily the pilot was Gary Forman, because he was the gentlest flier. He lifted straight up and while Gerry was watching the rope tighten up, the horizontal ice axe hooked into the armpit of his pile jacket. When the helicopter lifted off, there was Gerry hanging under the helicopter on nothing but the ice-axe pick. About three metres above the narrow ledge they had been standing on, the flap that held the ice axe to the pack broke and Gerry fell back down. If the pilot had not lifted straight up, Gerry would have had a couple thousand feet to fall before he landed.

I always felt a bit of relief once the army guys left.

Mount Robson
and Berg Lake.

9

THE SIDEHILLGOUGER SAYS,

"The climbers' theme song is: Please help me, I'm falling....

The theme song for a person caught in an avalanche is:

I've got a terrible feeling, everything is going my way...."

MOUNT ROBSON WAS always a very special mountain to me. It measures 3,954 metres tall, the highest in the Canadian Rockies, but due to the relatively low height of land on which it sits, this measurement does not truly reflect its size. Instead, the just over 3,000 metre vertical base to summit lift says more. In comparison, 4,389 metre Mount Elbert in Colorado, US, has a more gradual 1,615 metre elevation gain. Most mountains in the Rockies can be summited and descended in a single day, but in a day on Mount Robson a climber merely manages to reach the halfway point, with the summit and descent still ahead.

Due to its height and size compared to the mountains surrounding it, Robson generates its own weather. There are many days when the sky is perfectly clear and blue everywhere except around the peak of Robson, and in the shadow of the mountain there are plants growing that cannot be found anywhere else in the Rockies. The quickly changing weather patterns make the window for climbing it quite small, generally from mid-July to the end of August. A technically difficult mountain to climb at the best of times, special hazards that are rarely seen anywhere else, such as the snow Hoodoos near the top and the Black Ledges, add to the challenge.

I have stood on the summit of Mount Robson seven times in sixteen attempts, have spent numerous days training wardens there and have been involved in several difficult rescues. After a particularly demanding warden school on the mountain one year, Marv Miller said it best when he commented, "Boy, Willi, you brought home a bunch of humbled guys." Mount Robson is a humbling mountain.

When I first climbed Mount Robson, one of the most difficult and dangerous parts of the ascent was the section just past the summit of Little Robson. At that time, the preferred route was to go through what was called the Hourglass, behind Little Robson Peak, then get onto the glacier above and continue up. This was a very hazardous route and I never liked it.

It was nearly impossible to travel through that section of the Hourglass underneath the hanging ice of the glacier in reasonable safety. Climbers were forced to spend considerable time in the totally exposed gully, while large chunks of ice regularly broke off of the glacier above them. The ice chunks would barrel through the gully, knocking down loose rocks on the way and hitting anything in their path.

I figured there must be a better way. So one time, I made a camp on Little Robson and spent three days looking for a solution. I ended up finding a route, which was not very obvious but actually quite safe. It was quite a distance below the regular route, in an almost vertical section of the Hourglass, where the large ice chute was divided into two smaller gullies with a ridge in the middle. I found I was reasonably well protected from the falling ice on both sides of the divided chute. Conveniently, the centre ridge had a small ledge where a person could stand beneath an overhang, which provided protection from the falling ice and rocks.

The Black Ledges.

I timed the ice falls and came to the conclusion that it took nine to eleven seconds for a piece of ice to fall from the glacier to the chute I was standing beside. If you hustled, it took seven seconds to move across each chute from one safe place to the next. Working as a team, one climber could watch the glacier for falling ice and tell his or her partner when to go, and the partner would move quickly to the next safe place. It would be safer and easier to remove our climbing ropes to cross these two chutes.

The rocks in the area were black in colour, so I named the place *Die Schwarzen Binder*, which in German means the black bands or trusses. Over time, the name was Anglicized to "the Black Ledges" or "the Schwarz Ledges."

For first-time climbers on that route, the place was actually quite difficult to find. You had to go much lower than you expected to. Several times people came back from a Robson attempt saying that they were unable to find the ledges. I always asked if they were sure they went low enough.

I hauled the wardens through that place a few times, so they got to know the ledges well (where they were on the route and how to cross them). This specific training and knowledge of the mountain really saved our bacon a number of times during difficult rescue situations.

I remember during one of these warden climbs that one guy was standing on the ledge of the middle ridge ready to come out from below the overhang and run towards me, when suddenly the glacier above gave out a loud groan and a huge chunk of ice broke off. I hollered, "Stay back!"

He retreated under the overhang and then disappeared from view. The avalanche of broken ice, rocks and dust flowed over and around him. As usual for this section of the climb, he was not roped up. We had a few tense moments waiting for the dust to clear, wondering if he had gone down with the slide, but in the end, nothing happened. He was perfectly safe under that overhang in the middle of the chute.

Another huge challenge for climbers on Mount Robson is what the Alpine Club of Canada calls the Mushrooms, but I have always referred to as the Hoodoos. These are huge snow formations that look like vertical seracs or cornices, but instead of resulting from blowing wind, they are formed by the actions of Robson's unique weather patterns on snow deposits.

The Hoodoos can be anywhere from five to fifteen metres in height and, like a big noodle, form a full circle around the summit of the mountain. The most dangerous ones are on Emperor Ridge though. It is impossible for climbers to avoid the Hoodoos if they want to reach the top.

On the outside, the Hoodoos are covered with about an inch of ice, but if you push your fist through, the inside is all snow — powdery snow. How do you climb straight up through powder snow? You have no purchase whatsoever to climb it. More than a few climbers have had to turn back or have been stranded by the Hoodoos.

FACING

The Black Ledges
in poor weather.

ABOVE

The Hoodoos.

SUSANNA PFISTERER   191

The only solution for the Robson Hoodoos is to make a type of tunnel, like a chimney. You dig your way up, making sure that you burrow in far enough so that you can brace yourself against the snow. Not done properly or with bad luck, these Hoodoos can cause some serious trouble.

This became particularly evident one day when the rescue team was called out to look for two missing climbers. These two climbers had started off with some friends and made it up to the Robson Hut. The next day they decided to attempt the summit via the Wishbone Arête while their friends remained at the hut. When the climbers had not returned after two days, their friends descended the mountain and alerted us.

The Hoodoos start up by the Wishbone, so we had a pretty good idea of what may have caused the two men problems. We immediately called the helicopter and went in search for them.

When we reached the Wishbone near the bottom of the Hoodoos, we searched for the climbers. They were not there, but we did not have to look any further than the snow right in front of us to figure out what had happened and where they were. We could see that one guy had shovelled part way up a Hoodoo, building a chimney. Likely not braced securely enough, he fell. The indentation on the sloping, snow-covered ledge below the Hoodoo he was shovelling into was clear evidence of where he made impact. The fall most likely knocked him silly, as there were no marks in the snow indicating that he had tried to stop himself from sliding off the ledge. His slide path ended at the point where the northwest face of the mountain began.

Almost parallel to his slide path, you could see where his partner had stood belaying him, where the rope had tightened up and where he had been pulled off his stand. It was very clear where the guy went into self-arrest position—where he had jammed his ice axe down in an attempt to hold the whole damn thing. But the snow was just too soft to get a hold. The skid marks from his feet and his ice axe were imprinted in the snow as he got pulled over the edge.

So we flew down the mountain to look for what we knew would be bodies. We found one guy lying on the rocks in some narrows, while the other had come to rest on a snow cone. They had fallen a distance of more than 1,000 metres and were obviously both dead.

Right away we slung out the climber who had landed on the snow, but the other guy was tightly jammed into the rocks with ice having already formed around him. One of the wardens had to chop the ice free. The rope connecting the two climbers had broken in the accident, which was a hell of a thing considering a climbing rope has an 1,800-kilogram tensile strength.

It was a really tragic incident because the guy belaying did things correctly, but just could not hold himself or his partner due to the softness of the snow. Seeing the progression of events laid out in front of us like a mural was difficult for our team to absorb.

In the summer of 1984, I was conducting a warden school in the Maligne backcountry when I got the call over the radio that some climbers were overdue on Robson. It was reported that one of the missing climbers was Nicholas Vanderbilt, a younger member of the American Vanderbilt family and an heir to its fortune. The men had attempted an accent on the Wishbone Arête a couple of days earlier, but had not returned.

The weather that day and the day before was extremely poor — it was raining heavily and the sky was socked in to almost the valley bottom. We knew that higher up on the mountain this rain would have frozen to the rocks, resulting in a treacherous layer of verglas, and as the temperatures decreased, this ice would have been topped off by as much as a metre of snow.

Nevertheless, Gerry Israelson called the helicopter, piloted by Todd McCready, and with a couple other wardens flew up and looked for the missing climbers. Todd did his best to get in there, but every time they tried to fly higher up the mountain, the weather stopped them. After searching for some time, they returned to the base.

We knew that given the blizzard conditions, to send a rescue team up the mountain on foot with a very limited idea where on the huge mountain the climbers were, would have been almost totally useless. Due to Robson's enormous surface area, coupled with such poor visibility that would not have allowed the rescue team to see much more than a metre in front of them, it would have been a needle-in-a-haystack situation. In addition, the risk to the team was huge. We knew that if the two climbers were alive, they would be holed up in some snow cave or rock crevasse somewhere to wait out the storm.

By that night, I had made it out from Maligne and several members and friends of the Vanderbilt family, including Nicholas's mother, had flown up from Boston. We set up a meeting with them in the nearby town of Valemount, BC, which, given the stress of the situation, turned out to be very strained. Nicholas's uncle was angry that there was no team on the mountain looking for the men. I tried to explain how dangerous that would be.

I pointed out, however, that the weather forecast for the following day was much better and that we would be out there at dawn to resume the search.

It was decided during the meeting that a second helicopter would be brought into the search, paid for by the family. If the men were alive and holed up somewhere on the mountain, they would surely come out and signal their position when they heard the helicopters. I also had to tell the family that if the climbers were not alive, it would probably be very difficult to find the bodies, given the amount of rain and snow that had fallen.

So at six o'clock the next morning we started flying at sixty metre intervals, combing the whole mountain in search of the two men. I flew in one helicopter on the south side of Robson, and the other machine flew the north and west sides. Although we knew the intended route of the climbers, we didn't know if they had been on the ascent or descent of their climb at the point when they ran into trouble; thus we thoroughly searched the entire mountain.

By late afternoon, there was no sign of them. Nicholas's uncle sat in the back seat of the helicopter that I was in, and as the afternoon wore on and we still hadn't found any sign of his nephew, he slid further and further down into the seat and began to cry. It was a very difficult situation. By the end of the day, we realized that there was no chance of finding them alive.

We landed at rescue headquarters, where Nicholas's mother was waiting, to let her know the situation. I told her that Nicholas and his climbing partner were last seen a couple of days earlier near the Wishbone. While flying, we had noticed an avalanche deposit in a big gulley just below that area. More than likely, what had happened was that the two men had climbed up from the Wishbone through a very steep section. When they reached the flat part above, they probably released an avalanche, which knocked them down backwards.

I hesitantly asked her if she would like to fly up see for herself where her son was last seen. She told me she would, but she was deathly afraid of flying in small aircrafts. Then she turned, looked me in the eye and said, "You know, you look like the mountain itself. I think if you fly with me, I'll go."

So with tears running down her face, she sat in that helicopter, holding my hand, because that was the only way she would fly. We flew around and I showed her where the avalanche had released and where the deposit was, a long ways down, and explained again what most likely had happened. I said that in the fall, when the snow receded to its furthest point, we would have another look for her son. She said that whatever I needed in terms of helicopter time, she would foot the bill, but I never took her up on her offer.

That fall, I did fly around one day, searching that same stretch of mountain, but to no avail. As I sat in the helicopter, another avalanche released and fell into the same area. With rocks and avalanches regularly being funneled down into where the deposit lay, there was no way I could physically go into that area, or send anybody else in. It was a death trap. I could not jeopardize another life.

Due to the fame of the Vanderbilt name, early on in the rescue, the news media were on the scene and that resulted in all kinds of stories, some based on fact and some completely wild.

One story was that Nicholas was climbing with a guy that he
didn't really know and had never climbed with before. They said
his regular partner had not arrived yet, and he was so eager to
climb that he decided to go with this other guy. Of course, this
would be a dangerous thing to do, particularly on such a difficult mountain, and given that in climbing, you have to trust your
partner with your life. In truth, I don't know how well Nicholas
and his climbing partner knew each other or whether they had
climbed together before, but it did take some time to confirm the
identity of the second climber.

A momentary
break during a
rescue/recovery.

Another story that emerged was that Nicholas and his partner were making a TV show whereby the whole thing, from the start of a climb to the accident, was staged. According to this story, they would use actual footage taken of the rescue to complete the show. For a while it was rumored that the two men had already left the mountain and were hiding out somewhere waiting for the rescue to be completed. Obviously a complete fabrication, this story created nothing but painful feelings for the families.

On September 1, 1986, I spent my sixtieth birthday organizing a challenging rescue on Robson while participating in several other "situations" at the same time. It all started when four young guys from Jasper and Edmonton attempted to climb the north face of Robson. They were experienced ice climbers, so as long as the technical ice and rock climbing of the north face persisted, they would have been fine. But things changed when they reached the snow Hoodoos, which, as I have said, have stopped many climbers in their path. The weather had worsened, making the vertical twelve-metre Hoodoos above them particularly dangerous, and a retreat down the mountain also very difficult. In addition, one member of the team, they told us later, was sick. Given the conditions, they probably did the smartest thing they could — they sat there and did not move. After three days, the brother of one of the guys came to me and explained that the four climbers had not yet returned from their climb.

Mount Robson sits within the boundaries of a BC provincial park bearing its name, which at the time, meant that the RCMP from nearby Valemount had jurisdiction over any rescues in that area. However, Parks Canada had an agreement to perform technical rescues given that the skill set required was clearly beyond the scope of the small number of police stationed in Valemount. The RCMP were still part of the team though.

We called for the helicopter, which arrived quickly, flown by pilot Todd McCready. We tried to fly to where the men had been spotted but the weather started to close in. The climbers were near the top of the mountain, which would have been difficult to access by machine even in the best of conditions, given the helicopter's just over 3,000 metre-elevation operational limit. Todd managed to get a group of three wardens up onto the Kain route, which was still quite a distance from where the climbers were situated. In the meantime, a team of wardens from Banff joined the search and brought a more powerful helicopter with them. As they flew around on the south side, the weather cleared up a little bit and the pilot was able to put those three wardens on the far side of the Schwarz Ledges. Lastly, we put a third group of rescuers into the Robson Hut. The members of these three teams were all very experienced mountaineers and rescuers. I remained on the radio at the headquarters we established in the parking lot at the bottom of the mountain, acting as the base rescue leader.

Now we had one group of rescuers higher up on the mountain, one group on the Kain route and the other down by the hut. The members of the first group decided to climb that night in attempt to reach the stranded climbers. This group of Banff wardens was not as familiar with the mountain, so as I sat in the parking lot down below, Clair Israelson kept radioing down to ask where to go next.

Clair would say something like, "You know there is this big overhanging thing above me. Where do we go now?"

I replied, "Go to the right. There is a crevasse on the left side."

So they got through the crevasse area, basically went straight up and came to an ice face about an hour later. Then Clair radioed down, "There are two sets of tracks, one goes to the right and one goes to the left."

I answered, "Don't go to the right. Go a little bit to the left and then straight up. It's steep, but it's the best way to get out of there."

They did this and next I hear, "It looks like we're on the ridge now. The snow is soft here."

I said, "Turn to the left and head a little ways downhill. You'll come to a crevasse. Pass by this and go a short distance up to another crevasse."

A number of minutes went by before I heard from them again. "Gee, I don't know," said Clair. "We saw one crevasse and passed it, but now it doesn't seem to go anywhere anymore. We're on a flat area and it drops down in every direction."

I asked, "Well, was there a crevasse to the right? Did it have big icicles in it?"

"Yes," he replied.

"Yah, well," I said, "you screwed up. You're on top!"

They were standing on the summit at midnight with the four guys waiting to be rescued a few hundred feet below them on the other side.

I suggested the rescuers go back down to the crevasse and see if they could shelter there, which they did. The next day, they went over top of the mountain and a little ways down the other side and made contact with the four climbers. Then they threw a rope down from above and hauled up each guy over the hoodoos. After that, the group of them walked over the summit again, to the south side of Robson and down about 250 metres in altitude. But there they found their way was blocked. Since it was afternoon by that time, they made a bivouac in a large crevasse and stayed put. Meanwhile, I sent Gerry Israelson and his team up from the intermediate camp to break trail in order to help those guys get down.

The weather had been poor and socked in all day, but then, by some freaky bit of luck, it cleared enough, just barely enough, to let Todd fly in there and get them. As Todd flew up, he noticed another climber on the mountain who seemed to be lost. He took note of where that climber was, but continued on his way.

I had been out of contact with the four climbers and three rescuers for a while since they were holed up and we needed to conserve radio batteries. Finally, when the helicopter arrived, they turned the radio back on to talk to us. I said to the four rescued guys directly, "If you want a lift, here it is."

So they scrambled out of the hole, and two of them were put into the sling harness and hooked beneath the helicopter. Todd flew them down to the hut and then flew back up for the second two. By the third trip up the helicopter needed fuel.

I could hear the rescuers and pilot talking on the radio, suggesting that if the three rescuers hooked themselves in and then ran down the hill a ways just as the pilot lifted off, he could get them all down before he went for fuel.

I interfered and said, "You are at more than 3,600 metres elevation right now. Don't take any risks. I mean, shit, we got those four guys out of there and nobody's in danger at this point. Just take one person for now." So the pilot slung out one rescuer and went for fuel. Sure as hell the weather closed in again and the pilot couldn't fly back up. So Clair and Gord Irwin were stuck up on the mountain for another night and forced to bivouac.

Meanwhile, the rescuers who were initially dropped off at Robson hut had made it down the mountain themselves. The second group, consisting of Gerry Israelson, Greg Horne and John Neidre were, however, still en route below the hut.

The next day was my actual birthday. The four climbers had been rescued and were safe, but five rescuers were still on the mountain. It was totally socked in, right down to the base of Robson. I talked to the guys still on the mountain and knew what was going to happen next, as it had many times before. The guys would experience a huge letdown, which sometimes can be the most dangerous part of a rescue. They were discouraged as hell. I could hear it in Clair's voice over the radio. I said, "Now just watch it here. Go and lie down, sleep a little while. You got the job done; now we have to get you down safely."

On the day that followed the rescue, as we were trying to get our guys down, a man ran into the headquarters in the parking lot and said that there was a woman at Whitehorn Cabin with a broken leg. Situated halfway up the well-known Berg Lake hiking trail, which skirts the base of Mount Robson, the cabin was easy to reach. When the weather lifted slightly, the helicopter went in to pick her up.

As stated earlier, the RCMP had jurisdiction over rescues in Mount Robson Provincial Park and therefore, they were present at the rescue headquarters at the base of the mountain. Not long after we flew the woman out from Whitehorn, a call came in that there was a fatal vehicle accident on the highway about twenty kilometres from where we were. One of the policemen had to leave and attend to that incident. Then another call came in — there had been a murder in Valemount! This was probably the only murder in Valemount in thirty years. So off went a second policeman to deal with that.

A few hours later, another call. A small plane had crashed at Decoigne warden station at the west gate of Jasper National Park.

While all this was going on, the rescuers on the mountain had started to climb down. The weather was very bad and conditions were treacherous, but slowly, the upper group made their way down to the lower group who had already secured a rope into the Black Ledges. Together, they made it through the ledges and down to the cabin where they could be picked up if the weather cleared a bit.

Next, a guy named Rutherford came rushing into the headquarters. His story: "I upset my river raft on the Fraser River not far above Overlander Falls and there are still two people in the water."

Everyone in the room looked at each, starting to ask ourselves what terrible thing could possibly happen next. Obviously we needed to act quickly, so I directed the one team of rescuers that was already off the mountain: "You take the climbing ropes, the harness and two radios and go over to the river. Put the seat harness on."

I said to the pilot, "You get the helicopter ready and I'll reattach the cable underneath." This way we would be ready for another sling rescue.

So everybody flew in every direction. Brian Wallace strapped into the harness, was slung under the helicopter, and once at the river, plucked one of the rafters, who was holding onto a rock near the middle of the river, out of the water and onto shore. On the ground, the other rescuers roped one warden up who then jumped in and swam/floated down to the second rafter, who was hanging onto a windfall that was almost reaching the waterfalls. The rescuer got a hold of the guy on the windfall, and then the men on shore dragged them both back to safety by pulling on the rope. The policeman commented afterwards that the men in the river wouldn't have made it if the rescue hadn't been so quick. They were definitely in serious danger.

I was still at the headquarters trying to keep tabs on everything. Radio communication between the river rescuers and me didn't work because they were in a hole. So we communicated via the guys up on the mountain — one rescue team to another and then back down to me.

While up on the mountain, the rescuers met a guide named Tommy Hill who was there with a client. Tommy told them the client was causing him a lot of problems. We figured out that this client was the man that Todd had noticed earlier, looking somewhat lost.

That evening, I told our five guys still halfway up the mountain about the plane crash at Decoigne and about the other events of the day. John Neidre, who lived at Decoigne warden station, immediately asked, "Were any horses killed?" I had no answer for that.

The next day, the five wardens were on their way down, come hell or high water. As it happens, Gary Forman from Yellowhead helicopters in Valemount, a pilot who had also flown many difficult rescues for us, flew by. Over the radio he told us that he had an aviation inspector with him and they were en route to the plane crash site. On his return, I knew the guys up on the mountain couldn't hear what Gary was saying due to radio interference, but they could hear me. So I asked, "How did it go?"

He replied that it had been okay. So I asked, "How many horses were killed?"

He said, "Horses? There were no horses killed."

And I said, "Oh, really? That many?"

Poor Neidre up there on Robson, all he could hear was my side of that conversation.

The one hitch as the team continued to make its way down was that in the rush to get the four rescued climbers off the mountain a couple of days earlier, Gord Irwin's crampons were accidently taken down in the helicopter. As the weather closed back in, it rained, which then froze, making the ground a sheet of ice. The ice, in turn, was covered by a layer of fresh snow. And yet despite these conditions, Gord managed to make it down the mountain without crampons. They had to come through the ledges, in fog, snow and wind. In order to move fast, they left the tent up there along with some static climbing ropes in place.

Before the team left the hut, they handed one of their radios to Tommy Hill in case he ran into more trouble with his client. Sure enough, hours later, just as we were gathering our equipment up at the headquarters, we heard an accented voice coming over the radio. "Does anybody answer this radio?"

I told him about the conditions our guys had encountered below and advised him to stay at the hut for as long as he wanted. He and his client could eat whatever was in the hut and stay there until conditions improved. If I remember correctly, we still had to look for him a few days later.

That rescue of the four climbers was one that everyone involved will remember forever. We did get the four guys out of there alive under extremely difficult conditions. The rescue team climbed the highest mountain in the Rockies at night. And we did all that with minimum manpower. That was my thing you know — exposing as few people as possible to dangerous conditions, but utilizing the best people available. In addition, we had a murder case, an airplane crash, a river-raft rescue, a fatal car crash, a woman with a broken leg on a hiking trail and a second climbing party in difficulty — all in a day's work. Everyone did a great job.

Todd McCready was outstanding in his ability to pick those four climbers off Robson at an altitude of 3,718 metres in the howling wind flying a helicopter that had a just over 3,000 metre operational limit. At one point the wind was so strong it blew a lens right out of Gerry Israelson's glasses. Todd was nominated for helicopter pilot of the year after that, and he received the citation for it in Texas some time later.

When we finally returned to Jasper, I had some paperwork to finish off at the office. The wardens that had driven back with me went to my home to wait, to decompress and to have a beer. The biggest disappointment of the entire week was that for my birthday, my daughter Eva had attempted for the first time to make me my absolute favourite dessert — real Austrian *apfelstruedel*. It must have been good because by the time I arrived home, those guys had polished the whole damn thing off!

A river of ice,
Kluane
National Park.

10

THE SIDEHILLGOUGER OFFERS FOR RENT:

One snow cave: Good seasonal accommodation.

Standard features include wall-to-wall snow

and a basic white colour.

IN 1970, Kluane National Park was established in the south-west corner of Yukon Territory. Encompassing 22,013 square kilometres of the Saint Elias Mountains, the park is as big as all of Canada's other mountain national parks combined and includes Mount Logan, Canada's highest mountain, among its many giant peaks. In addition to its rugged mountains, the park features numerous glaciers, which, in some cases, measure more than one hundred kilometres in length and, in other cases, are among the fastest moving in the world. With almost half of its land mass permanently covered with ice and snow, Kluane's icefields are the largest outside of the polar icecaps. The area is plagued by some of the worst weather in North America, brought about largely by moist air moving up from the Gulf of Alaska, which blows up against the mountain range and results in huge quantities of snowfall. Due to its remoteness, it is not surprising that the area was largely unexplored at the time it was made a national park.

When the park was first established, I was asked to make a public safety plan as quickly as possible and then to set up a public safety/rescue program. This presented me with a number of challenges.

First of all, though there had been climbers in the area for quite some time, mountaineers are not known to be mapmakers.

Only because I had climbed Mount Logan eleven years earlier, it was likely that within Parks Canada I was the person most knowledgeable of that region. But that certainly didn't give me any understanding of the remaining huge area of Kluane Park. Canadian authorities had not yet made any attempts to map out the area either. In fact, at that time, the only people who had reasonable knowledge of the area were two men from Boston named Walter Wood and Bradford Washburn. They worked for the National Geographic Society, and years earlier had made a few expeditions into the area, mapping it out. In addition, Washburn had produced the first comprehensive set of aerial photographs of the region. Therefore, when the park came into existence, we had to phone or write to Boston in order to gain information about our own mountains. That was something I felt I had to change immediately.

Secondly, the park was so new that staff and infrastructure were not yet in place. What if a rescue was needed immediately? One of the things I did in that first year was travel up to Whitehorse and bring together all of the mountaineers already living in the area, to see who might be available at a moment's notice in case of an emergency in the mountains. I ran two one-week schools — one on rock and one on the glacier — with the small group of climbers I had found. There were not many people to draw from and as a result, the camps were not very successful. Only two guys could ski and the others used snowshoes. Interestingly, the two skiers went on to become successful guides in the area. From those schools it became clear that the best option was to work as quickly as possible to get a warden rescue team in place.

While Parks Canada was setting up offices and gathering staff, including wardens, I worked out a plan. The $25,000 dollars I was granted to spend on the public safety end of things wouldn't get you very far these days, but at the time it got us going. I went ahead and bought complete high-altitude equipment for ten men, from balaclavas right down to insulated triplex boots, skis and crampons, as well as camp equipment such as tents, stoves and sleeping bags. I also bought all of the rescue equipment necessary: cable set, Akja (a rescue sled), winches, heli-rescue seats, first aid supplies, Ambu Great (for respiratory support etc.) — everything required for a team to do its job in the difficult conditions of the Saint Elias. Later on, as time went by and we became more familiar with the conditions of the Saint Elias, I designed some stuff to fit our needs. The warmest type of sleeping bags, for example, were mummy bags, but they were not very comfortable given the weeks at a time we spent using them. The mummy bags forced you to keep both legs together, and we wanted something a bit roomier but without adding too much weight. We also made some modifications to the tents and other equipment we used; I told the manufacturers what we wanted and they complied, offering the designs for sale to the public soon afterwards.

That first year, I contacted a local helicopter company and set up an agreement to use their helicopters and pilots for rescues. Of course this meant spending time to train with the flight crew. One huge challenge was that the height of land in Kluane required pilots to fly at a minimum altitude of 3,300 metres to approach the park's interior. That was almost the ceiling for the Jet Ranger helicopter we used at first. Another challenge was the distances involved — an hour of helicopter flight time barely got us to the centre of the Park.

The next thing to establish was experience in the mountains — to cross the glaciers, to climb the mountains and to learn all about this new piece of Parks Canada real estate. So over the next number of years, the wardens and I did just that. The first warden expedition I set up was on the West Ridge of Logan the following year. Then every second year after that I organized and carried out two- to four-week expeditions to climb one or more of the higher mountains in the Saint Elias range. In the years between those major climbs, I put on smaller expeditions (a minimum of two weeks in length) that involved extensive rescue practices and glacier travel. All together, we participated in seventeen expeditions of one sort or another while I was there. We climbed most of the tallest mountains, and in a relatively short period of time many experienced and well-informed wardens became ready to do whatever was necessary to safely pull off the numerous hair-raising rescues we were involved in.

In those early years, we established numerous base camps in safe places for mountaineers to use (located far enough down the mountains to avoid being wiped out by avalanche). We also developed plane and helicopter landing sites. Our yearly expeditions helped us to get to know the terrain, the conditions and the routes of the area, and in turn gave us the ability to advise climbers entering the park.

One component of the public safety plan was to incorporate safety for expeditions, and thus we set up strict mountaineering guidelines. All expeditions were required to have: a minimum of four people in their party; appropriate equipment (a list of requirements was given to prospective climbers); a minimum amount of food (calculated by multiplying the number of team members by the length of trip and adding a reserve in case of an unplanned delay); and a radio. They could rent the radios from us if need be. Expedition teams needed to register for a trip with the wardens at least three months in advance and have documentation that each member of the group had passed an extensive doctor's medical test.

As I said, the first high altitude warden expedition was on the West Ridge of Mount Logan. I asked sixteen of the top guys from all of the mountain national parks in Western Canada if they wanted to take part and all sixteen accepted.

Everyone, including myself, then underwent an extreme medical checkup at the Foothills Hospital in Calgary to make sure that we were in adequate physical and mental condition to endure the stresses of arctic mountaineering. The information that I sent to the doctors before our checkup made it clear that climbers would be carrying twenty-five to forty kilo loads at altitudes between 3,000 and 6,000 metres for several weeks in possibly very low temperatures (–40°c) and high winds. Prolonged confinement in cramped tents or snow caves due to bad weather could also occur.

One doctor there had a special interest in strenuous high-altitude activity and he ran everybody through a series of aerobic fitness, endurance and physiological tests that included blood testing, treadmilling, and lung capacity. In the two days that we were at the hospital, the medical staff established a baseline and several testing regimes that were used to examine us several times in the years to come.

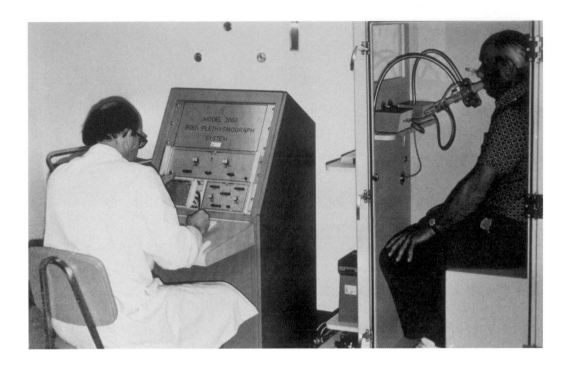

One of the recommendations of the Foothills medical team was to take a pill called Diamox during the expedition, for the prevention of altitude sickness. This was controversial. German doctors who had studied it did not recommend its use. I personally felt any kind of pill was a crutch. We did end up using it, and some members of the team later stated they felt it helped a lot.

In the end, ten men were chosen to take part in that first expedition. The plan was that one guy would remain at base camp and assist with the initial part of the trip. Once his job was complete, he would then fly out from the base by helicopter. In groups of three, the other nine men would attempt to climb the mountain.

To make sure the rescue team was healthy, we spent a lot of time blowing into tubes and sucking out of them.

The King Trench Route on the West Ridge of Mount Logan was actually the route most often used by climbers to reach the summit of the mountain. I approached the trip with the goal of testing the men and the equipment, and that goal was certainly achieved due largely to the terrible luck we had with the weather. In the three weeks we were on the mountain, we only had two-and-a-half days of reasonably good weather — the rest of the time we were faced with severe blizzard conditions and extreme cold. A lot of the time, the wind was blowing at a rate of 100 to 130 kilometres per hour, while the temperatures dipped into the −40 range. We made it to the plateau at 5,300 metres, but had to quit there and did not reach the summit.

FACING

West Ridge of Mount Logan.

ABOVE

When it's 40 below and the wind is blowing at 100 km/hr, even going to the outhouse is a memorable experience.

What we learned from that experience was that on the west or Pacific Ocean side of the Saint Elias Mountains, the weather is generally far more severe than on the eastern slopes. During those three weeks of attempting to climb the West Ridge in blizzard conditions, the East Ridge of the mountain experienced nothing but beautiful (albeit cold) blue-sky weather. Looking back on the trip, I bet our team had the strongest skill and knowledge level to have hit Mount Logan back then. That was quite a group of guys.

A few years later, we had organized an expedition to climb Mount Hubbard and Mount Kennedy. To access the two mountains, we approached via the Cathedral Glacier, which is a glacier on the move! The crevasses would close and open so quickly that one day you would notice a huge crevasse in a particular spot and the next day it was gone. The snow and ice were so broken up that we used up all of our wands just to mark the crevasses. We had a hell of a time just getting up to 3,300 metres where we were forced to make camp. We would have liked to camp at least 300 metres higher in altitude, but due to very difficult and time-consuming travel on the Cathedral Glacier, that was just not possible.

The problem was that we still had quite a stretch to go to reach the summits. Mount Kennedy was not too bad because it's only 4,250 metres in height, but Mount Hubbard is 4,557 metres (a 1,250 metre vertical lift from base camp). Normally, a 900 metre lift (for a summit bid) is about the right amount of change in elevation at such altitudes and oxygen levels.

So we climbed Kennedy the following day and had a good trip. It was a large group with nine guys (including myself), on three ropes. We climbed with short skis, except for the summit ridge where we left our trusty boards behind.

The next day, we went after Hubbard. Early on during the climb, we encountered deep snow in a couple of places, making travel difficult. Then when we got up onto the upper plateau, the snow conditions improved and we were able to make good time again. On the final ridge, we left our skis behind and climbed the rest of the way on foot with crampons strapped to our boots.

I was in the lead on that last ridge before the summit, and when I reached it, I turned and watched the guys come up to join me one after the other. I shook each of their hands, congratulating them on the successful climb. Everybody shook my hand in return but said nothing. Suddenly I realized that although there were eight men standing in front of me, they weren't *really* there. They were all out to lunch — a bunch of zombies — the lights were on but nobody was home.

So there I was standing on a 4,500-metre mountain with a bunch of unresponsive guys and we still had to descend. I realized we had overdone the whole thing and I got scared. What was I going to do to get them down safely?

After about ten minutes of standing at the summit, one guy suddenly said, "Hey, we're on top."

Then they all seemed to wake up and started to look around. Soon they were all exclaiming, "Oh we're on top," and congratulating each other. Boy, was I glad that the lights turned on and they came home!

We made it down to base camp without further incident and the next day we headed back down the glacier. I stayed behind a bit with my group that morning, in order to clean up the camp, while the other two groups went ahead. A heavy fog was sitting down below us and the two groups descended into it.

Suddenly from where we were, my group saw a huge chunk of the glacier break off. This caused a gigantic avalanche right above where the teams had disappeared into the fog. I thought: "Holy shit!"

As the avalanche disappeared into the fog, my team and I quickly headed off. Once we passed through the fog and beneath it, I could see the other guys on the flats in the distance moving down toward our next camp. What seemed like half the glacier had broken off on the east side, but luckily all three of our groups had been far enough to the west to avoid getting hit by it.

As time went on, more and more information became available about things like mountain sickness (pulmonary and cerebral edemas). Above an altitude of 3,000 metres, almost all mountaineers feel sick for a short while — early symptoms include persistent headaches, nausea, loss of appetite and sleeplessness. If the symptoms persist, however, and the climber also starts to experience breathlessness even at rest, a severe cough possibly with bloody or watery sputum and noisy, bubbling breathing, then edema has developed. Fluids settle in the lung(s) resulting in waterlogged lungs, and may develop in the brain as well (waterlogged brain/cerebral edema). Unless the patient is taken down to a lower altitude immediately, he or she will die.

At high altitudes, the oxygen content in the air in relation to nitrogen is similar to sea level ratios — twenty-one percent, but the density of the air is much less. In the St. Elias Range, the oxygen available to climbers is even lower than other places in the world of similar altitude, due to the vast icefields and the lack of vegetation for a hundred kilometres in every direction.

Finally we
had a roof over
our heads
(Mount
Alverstone).

A room with
a view
(Mount Steele).

In order to acclimatize to high altitudes and hopefully avoid altitude sickness, it was recommended at the time to make camp a maximum of only 450 vertical metres higher a day (nowadays 300 vertical metres is recommended). On the day of a summit bid, a 900 vertical metre climb is average, but teams return to the established high camp that evening.

When I planned trips, I made sure to take the threat of altitude sickness into account. For example, when deciding on a climbing route, I always made sure a quick downhill retreat was possible, because if someone developed signs of pulmonary or cerebral edema, we needed to quickly get that person a minimum of 900 vertical metres lower on the mountain.

When we were at higher altitudes, I also made a point of ensuring each team member was checked out twice a day for any indication of pulmonary edema by our designated team "doctor" (generally known as Dr. Nuisance). He would place a stethoscope between each person's shoulder blades, and listen. If he heard a gurgling sound, then we had to get that guy down the mountain. Pulse rates were also checked twice daily and monitored for any sign of changes. In a case of pulmonary edema, a person gets dehydrated as water content moves towards the middle of the torso (the lungs), and the lungs actually drown out with too much water. That water in the lungs makes a gurgling sound, so as soon as you hear that noise, the whole thing becomes very serious and possibly deadly.

If you do manage to get the person 900 metres lower, then the problem resolves itself. The only other thing that would help the situation is a pressure chamber, which obviously was not an option for us. So every time somebody did not sound quite right, down he went, often times under great protest.

One time we were at a camp on McArthur Peak and were planning to summit the more than 4,300 metre mountain the following day. The camp we were at wasn't actually that high, maybe 3,300 metres or so. Well guess who got sick? And guess who didn't want to go down the mountain?

That evening after supper I didn't feel well, so someone checked me out and heard a mild gurgling, but I insisted it was nothing and we all went to sleep. During the night it worsened, and by two o'clock in the morning, there was so much gurgling in my breathing that the people in the tent beside me were woken up. At that time of year it was almost daylight anyway, so they rolled me out of my sleeping bag, dressed me up, packed up the tent, and down the mountain I went. I had no choice in the matter anymore. And I am telling you, going down was really tough. Two guys had to help me the entire way. There was one place where we had to climb back up maybe a couple hundred feet before continuing our descent and, boy, was that difficult — I just didn't have any strength left. Slowly though, as we got further down, it became easier. With pulmonary edema, it doesn't matter how fit you are. If you have it, you must descend 900 metres within approximately twenty-four hours — otherwise you die.

On another trip, we were once again on the Cathedral Glacier, and once again, my gut feeling saved me. We had planned to climb a few mountains, but the avalanche hazard was too high, so we decided to travel across the glacier and practice rescue techniques instead. We went up a ridge and came to an avalanche deposit. The avalanche had descended through a gulley from the pitch above. We decided to have lunch there because generally on an avalanche deposit you don't have to worry about crevasses — the snow from the avalanche most likely had filled them up. After lunch, we planned to cross the rest of the deposit, and then once back on the glacier, find some open crevasses that we could use for rescue practice.

Gordy Peyto was the second guy on my rope that day. Usually, given the conditions, I would have tied into the rope and then walked until the rope between Gordy and me tightened up. Then he would have started off. That day however, I put the rope on and said, "Gordy, give me a belay."

Gordy stepped back and gave me a half-hearted belay, so I said, "No, give me a real solid belay."

I hadn't noticed anything odd or potentially dangerous about the snow conditions, so I am not sure why I insisted on that belay. Gordy shrugged, but got himself into a good solid position and tightened the rope up. I took about two steps forward and… down I went. Being in a good solid stance, Gordy held my fall and pulled me up.

Moments before when I had asked for the belay, the whole team had looked at me questioningly. There just couldn't be a crevasse in the avalanche deposit we were on. Yet somehow, as I found out, there was. What most likely had happened was that the avalanche deposit had been there for quite some time and the snow had settled down below in the crevasse, leaving a hole just

Ice blocks
(Mount Kennedy).

below the surface of the top layer of snow. I realized this after the fact. Beforehand though, I assumed everything was fine and that crevasses weren't even a concern, yet somehow my gut told me to ask for that belay. Why was I so insistent? In thinking about it later, I came up with only one answer: I have no idea.

My intuition didn't always tell me what I wanted to hear, but I listened to it anyway, and after a while the wardens trusted it too. In the early seventies when we first arrived at Kluane, all of the higher mountains in the Saint Elias range had already been climbed, but a few of the smaller ones had not. One year, while on yet another warden expedition, we climbed one such mountain near the Kaskawulsh Glacier. We were very close to the summit of what would have been a first ascent, but then my intuition told me something was wrong and to not go any further.

In terrain like this you're better off in the helicopter.

When I told the team this, nobody questioned me and we backed off, even though all of us would have loved to claim the first ascent. On the 28th of August, 1974, we did however, make a first ascent on Mount Southesk (3,124 metres).

A few years later, we put on an expedition up the East Ridge of Mount Steele. From the base of the mountain, we planned to make it to the summit of the 5,073-metre mountain in two camps. At the high camp, on the morning of the approach day for the summit, one guy cut his hand very badly on the lid of a tin can. The wound would not stop bleeding — at such a high altitude, blood does not clot as well as it normally would. So I decided to send a group of four toward the summit. In the meantime, we bandaged the guy's thumb up as best we could and then two guys downclimbed with him to a place where the helicopter could come and pick him up.

Oh my God,
2800 vertical
metres of this?

Ron Chambers, one of the wardens based at Kluane and a prominent member of the indigenous community in the Yukon, and I waited at the high camp to see how things developed. Everything went all right. The helicopter came to pick up the warden with the cut hand and his helpers while the other party made the summit.

Once things were sorted out with the injured guy, it was too late for Ronnie and me to attempt the summit, so we remained at the high camp that day. The climbers returned to the camp very late and told us that although they had reached the peak, it had been a tremendous struggle in very poor conditions. They were all really worn out. That night a bad storm moved in, so it was good they all made it down when they did.

At the camp, we had everything ready for them — hot tea and a warm supper. All they had to do was crawl into their sleeping bags and get comfortable. We served the dinner to them and afterwards I kept going around to their tents and filling their cups with tea. They relaxed and started to feel better. Then after midnight sometime, I went around once more to check on everyone, and out of this one tent I hear Darro Stinson say, "Thanks, Willi. Thank you very much for giving me the opportunity to climb this fucking mountain." I think most of the guys felt the same way about many of the mountains we climbed in the Saint Elias.

As you can imagine, over the years, we had many really wild rescues in the mountains of the Saint Elias. As visitation to the park increased, the accidents increased. Many times tragedy had already occurred before we arrived on scene, but we were also able to save people's lives on a number of occasions.

In what was a lucky break for us, a few years after the park was established, the helicopter company we used for rescues acquired a high-altitude Alouette with a winch. This helicopter was bigger and more powerful and could fly to higher altitudes than any of the previous machines. The winch could be used to get a person off a mountain above 3,600 metres, and to then pull the injured climber and rescuer up into the helicopter. Given the elevations we had to conduct these rescues at, and the extreme cold and long distances we had to cover to get out from the remote areas, it was not possible to leave the injured person or rescuer hanging beneath the machine on a long-line as we most often did in the other parks. More than anywhere, in the Saint Elias we needed to winch them up and bring them inside the machine to fly home.

It often seemed to me that in my career the team and I were just barely one step ahead of where we needed to be. This was really evident in Kluane that spring when we had access to the Alouette helicopter for the first time. We were able to use it on a Friday, so the Kluane team and I practiced for a number of hours. The following day, I had to return to the south, and that Sunday the team received a call to conduct a rescue at an altitude of over 4,000 metres. A climber on the East Ridge of Mount Logan had pulmonary edema and needed to be immediately evacuated.

I was alerted of the rescue right away and remained in radio contact with the team, but couldn't physically help them. As we spoke on the radio, the guys and I became suspicious of the situation. It seemed as though the climber's teammates had just left him at the camp, while they made a bid for the top. These suspicions were never verified, but at any rate, the guy remained at that altitude too long without being given help to descend.

The rescue team prepared themselves, called the helicopter and attempted to fly in. By two o'clock in the morning, the wind calmed down enough for the team to board the Alouette with pilot Ron Eland. They lowered Ron Chambers down to the sick man. Ronnie bundled him up and attached the stretcher to the cable to be winched up to the helicopter, all made possible by the midnight sun that allowed him to see what he was doing. Due to flying conditions, the helicopter could only lift one guy at a time, the first of whom would be, of course, the victim. So the pilot lifted him off the mountain. Luckily the weather held, so the pilot could return and pick up Ronnie, too. That was a real weak point in the operation though, because if for some reason the

One of seventeen expeditions.

helicopter could not have gone back, Ronnie would have been in major trouble at that high of an elevation without having acclimatized properly.

Later at the hospital in Whitehorse, the doctors informed us that the climber would have had only about two hours to live had he remained on the mountain. A week earlier, without use of the new helicopter, the team would not have been able to pull off that rescue.

Another time I was up in Kluane conducting a rescue school when we received a call that a party of climbers was stranded at about 4,500 metres on Mount Logan. They had been sleeping in snow caves when an avalanche came down and took their entire camp except the snow caves down with it. Luckily, they were safe, but they had no gear left. So we called the Alouette and flew into their location. Under normal circumstances this rescue would have been no problem, but it turned out to be one of those rare warm days with no wind, on which, at that altitude, the pilot could not hover the helicopter. We flew into the rescue site with Ronnie Chambers hanging underneath on an eighteen-metre cable. When the pilot, again Ron Eland, tried to hover near where the climbers were, he couldn't hold the machine steady — due to the weather conditions, he had no control. There was just not enough bite under the propellers at that high elevation to allow the machine to hover, so in order to avoid a crash, he had to dive forward to gain some speed and to regain control.

Ronnie meanwhile was hanging on the cable under the helicopter. As the pilot dove, Ronnie ended up directly horizontal behind the machine. Some rescuers who had been dropped off at a point lower down the mountain took a few photographs of

Edema rescue,
at 4100 metres
in 50-kilometre
winds.

Ronnie's wild ride. Once he gained control, the pilot tried once more to get to the rescue site, but it just wasn't going to work.

I radioed the climbers from inside the helicopter, telling them that we were unable to get into where they were and that they would have to move to a lower spot. At that point, one of them informed us that he was buck-naked. He had been sleeping in his sleeping bag with nothing on, not even underwear, when the slide had taken everything down. So I said, "Okay you guys, make a list of everything that you need and we will get it up to you. Once you have the stuff, make your way down to a lower elevation. We will try to pick you up tomorrow."

They made a list and radioed it to us. As it turned out, the guy who had lost everything was exactly my size. So we landed the helicopter lower down and proceeded to put a bag of stuff together with climbing gear, ropes, crampons, and some survival equipment like a stove, another radio, some food, and a pair of boots for another member of the climbing group. I took everything including my underwear off and sent it up in the bag for the naked guy. We tied it on a long rope, then flew by and dropped it all down to them. When they got it, we asked them to check the clothes and boots out to see if they fit and everything did.

It was getting late, so we had to leave. We were a hell of an outfit, flying out over the divide. If the helicopter had gone down, I would have been sitting on the glacier buck-naked myself with no equipment because those guys had everything of ours. The climbers were happy that they now had what they needed, and as a result, they made it down the mountain by themselves. When you start off to a rescue scene, you never know what you will encounter or what type of help will be needed. This was an example of a rescue that went in a different direction than expected.

We had another rescue up on Mount Logan, which involved a young guy who was the heir to the Maytag fortune. Apparently he and his three climbing partners had gone up the King Trench route. While two members of the group made a bid for the summit, this young guy and his partner set up camp and mistakenly put their tent too far out on a cornice. The cornice broke and they went down with the tent. When the other two came down from the mountain, they could clearly see what had happened. Those two guys had fallen a distance of about 2,000 metres.

The two remaining climbers reported the accident, first to authorities in Alaska and then to us, but by that time more than a day had passed. The wardens and I flew in from Kluane Park headquarters and when we arrived, we noticed another helicopter was already there. It had flown in from the nearby Alaskan town of Yakutat. On board were some Alaskan rescue officials as well as the climber's father and another son.

The wardens and Alaskan rescuers searched the area below the fall and saw something lying on the avalanche deposit. We slung in and found a rucksack, which turned out to be the one that belonged to the Maytag boy. The avalanche deposit was at least thirty metres deep, located in a draw that was too risky a place for a search team to go in and set up a probe line, especially given that there was absolutely no chance that the two men were alive. We informed the two family members of this and the father agreed, but the brother was very upset that we wouldn't do more. After some time, we had to depart flying east to Parks headquarters, while the Alaskan crew and the family members flew the shorter distance to Yakutat.

Once in the early seventies, we had a call that there had been an ice/snow avalanche on Mount Poland. The mountain didn't actually have a name at the time, but because the expedition that had called us was Polish, we started calling it Mount Poland.

The Polish climbers had been caught in an avalanche and one man was still missing. The Kluane wardens were not able to locate him, so they asked if Alfie and I could come up with our search dog, Ginger. We drove to Edmonton, took the noon plane to Whitehorse where they picked us up with the helicopter, and flew to Haines Junction. Our equipment was all laid out for us when we arrived, so we quickly changed into high-altitude gear and flew in to the avalanche site.

At that point, we were still using the Jet Ranger helicopter. We flew down the Alsek Glacier in perfectly calm, sunny weather. All of a sudden, for what seemed like no reason, the helicopter fell 360 metres in altitude and then lifted right back up again. Ginger was floating up on the ceiling of the helicopter during the drop. Afterwards, when they checked the helicopter out, the maintenance crew found that it had popped seventeen rivets and the motor mouth as a result of that drop. We didn't know that, so we continued to the rescue site.

From that point on, it became very windy. We came around the Alsek Glacier, then up the Cathedral Glacier and on to Mount Poland. Since it was so rough, the pilot could only fly one person at a time into the site of the accident, so I flew in first. He nosed into the site and I jumped out. I then tried to shovel out a better landing site while he went for the others. Soon Alfie and a few other guys had joined me.

This was an ice/snow avalanche where huge chunks of ice had come down with the snow. There was a small chance that some of the large ice blocks could have piled up against each other like a tepee leaving a space between them where a person could be trapped but alive. Time was of the essence though, as it had already been three days since the accident.

Alfie put Ginger to work and he indicated something almost immediately. We dug down and found a pile of shit. You can't blame the dog for that — it was a human smell. We continued the search and after a short while Ginger indicated very strongly near some of the largest ice blocks. We unsuccessfully tried to dig around in the area, but in order to get any further, we would have required chainsaws or chisels to get through the ice.

Again due to the remoteness of these mountains, to get those items would have involved a return flight of at least an hour and a half. Meanwhile, the pilot was getting more and more nervous because the weather was getting worse, the wind was increasing, and it was getting late. The weather forecast called for worse conditions the next day.

So we dug down as far as we could beside the giant ice block where the dog had indicated and found nothing. Then I crawled into the furthest recess of the hole and called out as loudly as I could. I sat in there for quite some time in silence and listened for any sound that may indicate that the guy was still alive and trapped. There was no sound, so we had to make the decision to give up.

We then had a hell of a ride flying out. Normally I was the last person to be flown out of a site, but in this case I went first. Larry Trembley, a Kluane warden, and a couple of other guys ended up spending the night there. The next morning, following another attempt to hear something at the rescue site, they too were flown out. They had a really rough ride in very strong winds coming out, and as a result, Trembley vowed never to set foot into another helicopter as long as he lived.

Sometimes the decision in respect to when to terminate a rescue is not clear and thus very difficult. With that particular rescue, the difficulty of chainsawing through huge blocks of ice in such a remote place with several risks facing the rescue team was huge compared to the chance of finding a man alive behind the ice chunks three days after the avalanche. Still, that was one rescue where I did question *what if*. What if the climber had still been alive in that debris somewhere and we gave up?

In Kluane National Park, the warden team (with and without my presence) pulled off numerous very difficult rescues in the harshest of conditions, without incident or injury. The public safety standards and the rescue program procedures that we conceived and implemented for the park still form the foundation of the program today.

The midnight sun.

Looking back
and ahead,
Mount Logan.

11

THE SIDEHILLGOUGER SAYS,

"You meet a mountain on its terms, not yours."

IN 1980, we again put a warden expedition on Mount Logan, this time on the East Ridge. More than twenty years later, there I was back on the East Ridge.

The goals of this high altitude orientation and rescue school were similar to the ones before it. They included, among others:

to work as a team toward a common goal

to expose men and equipment to the prevailing environment

to gather information about the mountain and surrounding glaciers in regard to climbing routes, difficulties, hazards, evacuation routes, communication and rescue problems

to organize and prepare for an expedition climb

to train and prepare for rescue missions

This time we flew to the base of the mountain. We started off with twelve men, but as we moved our gear up to the first camp, one member of our team was hit by a falling rock, so we had to call the helicopter to fly him out. Another guy decided to go with him, leaving us as a group of ten.

When we arrived at the first camp, I went up the mountain a ways with one of the guys to assess the conditions. We could immediately see that the start of our climb would be very difficult.

This time we had
a better sponsor.

Between the first and second camp is an extremely exposed ridge
with 2,000-metre drops on either side. This ridge was covered
with a sheet of ice. When we had climbed this section in 1959, it
had been covered in a layer of crusty snow, making it like a staircase (easy to walk on) but this time we wouldn't have such luck.

The ice had formed as a result of warm temperatures just
before we arrived at Logan. The snow on the ridge had melted
and then refrozen. We couldn't cut steps into the snow, as we normally would have, so instead we had to front-point all the way up
to the 4,300-metre level. That's where we set up Camp 2.

Due to conditions, we decided there was too much hazard for
ten guys to try to reach the summit, so we sent four up instead.
The rest of the guys would stay at Camp 1. Ron Chambers and
I helped the four guys who would attempt to summit by carrying a load up to Camp 2 for them and then headed back down.

It was midnight on a June day when we left Camp 2, but since there was still daylight, time didn't matter. Between midnight and two o'clock in the morning, the sky darkened a little but was never totally black.

Even though it was my choice to let the four guys go for the summit, it was a real sore point for me. I went off by myself for a while, feeling really down. It marked the first time in my career that I had to stand back and let someone else go ahead. I had always been the one in front, always in the lead, always getting the job done, and now I was to turn back and descend. It felt like a door had closed on me after all those years.

When Ronnie and I headed back down to Camp 1, there was a group ahead of us that were very slow. They were bothered by the steepness and the ice, but Ronnie and I just clambered down on front points.

The four guys continued on up the mountain. They established Camp 2, 3 and 4 and then made the summit, all four of them. That spring there were seven expeditions on the East Ridge, a huge number. One of the challenges our guys faced during their ascent was a bit of a traffic jam at the narrowest part of the climb.

On their way down, the weather worsened. The guys made it to Camp 2 but were socked in by fog. At Camp 1, where we were, the fog and clouds were above us. I relayed this information to them via radio. I told them that if they went down to the horizontal ridge and then slightly below, they'd be out of the fog and then able to downclimb the rest of the way with ease. They immediately packed up and descended. We climbed part way to meet them, put in a few ropes to help them down and before we knew it, we were all back at Camp 1.

As mountaineers, we were subject to the same pitfalls as others involved in dangerous situations. When a person is subject to high hazard for an extended period of time, he or she uses tremendous energy to remain alert and to concentrate on remaining safe. Then when the hazard eases up somewhat, the person lets down his or her guard. If, however, the danger has not completely disappeared, the potential for accidents in this lower state of alertness is high.

The four guys who had come off the summit had been on very difficult terrain — steep ice — in fluctuating weather conditions for six days and had navigated it safely. They had achieved their goal of summiting the mountain and were of course, proud of their accomplishment. When they rejoined us at Camp 1, they relaxed a little, knowing there was only one section of the mountain left to descend, and that section was certainly less hazardous than what they had come through.

The day after they rejoined us, all ten of us packed up the camp and continued down the mountain. We travelled in two-man teams with no blundering our way down — we were roped up properly, with crampons on and everything, except some guys walked with ski poles rather than their ice axe. I was in the lead.

There was about ten centimetres of new snow on the ridge with that ice layer underneath. As I walked across, I noticed a chute dropping off to one side and I thought to myself, "Boy, a guy would have to have a real talent to slide into this thing here."

I continued along and a short while later, one of the men behind me hollered, "Willi, Tim fell down. Peter fell down."

I thought they were fooling around, so I said, "Well, tell them to get up."

The guy says, "No, no, falling. They are falling off the mountain. Oh my God, they are still going."

Five of us had crossed safely past the chute, I had noticed a few moments before. The sixth guy, Tim Auger, who was actually the best mountaineer of the whole team, slipped and started to slide down. He didn't pay much attention, thinking he could hold himself or that his rope-mate, Peter Perren, would hold his fall. Instead, the rope tightened up and he pulled Peter off as well and down they went.

We could hear something rumbling, and I realized that yes, in fact, they were still falling. They flew most of the way down through the air hitting snow in the chute occasionally. I climbed a little forward and I could see the snow accumulating a little bit at the bottom of the gulley. I was looking right down between my feet, which made me realize how steep the drop actually was.

My first reaction was anger. "How the hell can anyone fall off there?"

Then the situation started to really sink in. For a few moments the group of us stood in silence while various thoughts raced through my mind and I am sure theirs as well.

"Okay, okay, first of all everyone hold still. It looks like they went all the way down."

"We are not far below Camp 1 at an elevation of 3,200 metres and the glacier is at approximately 2,600 metres. That is a 600 vertical metre drop. Nobody can survive that."

"Obviously we cannot downclimb the two guys' descent route, so we will have to follow the East Ridge down and then walk along the glacier for some distance to reach them. That will take at least four hours."

They fell 600 vertical metres down the centre chute to a small avalanche deposit.

Since the batteries of our VHF radios were almost dead at that point and hardly useable, I immediately sent three guys the short distance back to the plateau where Camp 1 had been situated and told them to set up the short-wave radio antenna. Once the radio was in operation, they were to try to contact somebody to get help. Those guys did what I asked and managed to make contact with somebody in Prince George, British Columbia almost immediatcly. They asked the person in Prince George to phone Kluane Park headquarters to alert them of the situation.

As they were talking, our helicopter pilot was searching for a frequency on his radio and by pure fluke happened to hear the conversation. That day he had been hired by a group that was making a film nearby. They had a helicopter of their own there, which he was flying. He immediately dumped the film crew and prepared to fly in to us.

As the remaining three of us stood on the ridge preparing to downclimb, one of the guys said, "Listen." Sure enough we could hear shouts from below. Someone was alive!

I climbed forward a few steps and between my legs I could see a fresh avalanche deposit on the glacier below and someone moving around.

"Hello. We're okay!"

Whoa. At first it was hard to believe that they had survived. Then I thought, "Yeah, they might be alive (although pretty beaten up) right now, but by the time we get down there it could be another story."

Ron Chambers, Tom Davidson and I started down the ridge. The going was tough and very slippery over snow-covered rocks. Once off the ridge, we planned to cross what looked like a difficult section of glacier, to try to get to the two injured climbers and to help them. A cirque of almost vertical rock faces surrounded them, made up of the east ridge of Logan on one side, the Hubsew Ridge on the other, and at the head, the 2,400 metre wall of Mount Logan. This huge hole is obviously a very hazardous place.

Three-and-a-half hours later, we arrived at a chute that led down to the glacier. Not knowing if the men above with the short wave radio had been successful in reaching someone, I decided to try the VHF radio once more. Maybe the batteries had recuperated enough to get something out of it. I turned the radio on and called to our helicopter pilot, Ron Eland. To my amazement he answered me. He told me he was already on the way, currently passing over the divide and flying towards us. He was flying the Alouette III, had warden Ray Frey with him, and a support helicopter (a Bell 204) was also on the way. When he arrived, he would first fly to base camp so that Ray could get additional rescue equipment from our cache.

As we continued our way down, the weather socked in below us. Although it had been clear that morning, now there was only one small beam of sunlight shining down to where the injured guys were, and the rest of the area including the entire East Logan Glacier and base camp was completely in the fog.

Ron Eland had landed at base camp just before the fog rolled in, but now could not fly because he had no visual reference. I was still a short distance up on the ridge and could see the depth of the fog. I kept telling him that if he lifted off, it was only about fifteen metres to get above it. He wouldn't do that at first, but eventually he skirted the machine about two kilometres up on the glacier and finally emerged out of the fog below us.

Once out of the fog, they sighted the victims and landed nearby between some big crevasses. Ray Frey tended to Tim and Peter, while the pilot flew over to where we were near the bottom of the ridge. He picked up Ron Chambers, the designated "doctor" for the trip, and also flew him over to the two guys to help.

As I watched the helicopter land at the accident site, the sun was still shining into that hole. I could see one of the injured guys sitting on the glacier waving at me. A short while later the helicopter was back in the air. As he buzzed by, Ron Eland radioed me to say, "It's okay. The guys are okay. We're on the way to the hospital now."

So while they flew out, Tom Davidson and I downclimbed the 300-metre chute. The bergschrund was open so we had to rappel. That was when, like so many times before, this syndrome hit again — post-traumatic stupidity. As always, when the emergency was all but resolved and the stress was relieved, that's when you were likely to make some stupid decisions. And I did.

We went a short distance down to where we had left a deposit of equipment and food and I said to Tom, "We have to move this out onto the glacier so the helicopter can pick it up." So we made three trips back and forth, lugging all the stuff. It was a completely useless thing to do. Tom tried to talk me out of it but couldn't. We wasted about an hour doing that and as a result almost jeopardized the helicopter ride out.

After moving the stuff around, we stomped the rest of the way down to base camp. There were quite a few crevasses, so we really had to watch where we were going. As we moved down into the fog, we could hear a helicopter below us. When we reached camp, the helicopter was waiting there. The pilot of the Bell 204 had picked the three guys off of Camp 1 and flown them down to base camp. Then they had packed and loaded up the camp while waiting for us to arrive.

As they waited, the pilot became increasingly nervous about our late arrival because he didn't want to lift off in the fog. It was not a dense fog at that point, sort of streaky, so he had some visibility every so often, but there was a strong possibility that it would close in more. When we finally showed up, everyone screamed and hollered, "Let's go, let's go."

Tom and I ran down the remaining distance to base camp, crampons and rope still on, and jumped right into the helicopter. They threw a few boxes on top of us and off we went.

The Bell 204 helicopter was an old clunker of a machine, and as we flew away the door was moving back and forth almost ready to fall off. We were used to the Alouette, which was like the Cadillac of helicopters at the time. It gave you a real smooth, quiet, easy ride. That rattling and clinking old Bell generally gave you anything but. Yet that day as I sat in there, what it did give me was an amazing feeling of security. We all flew out and then headed for the hospital in Whitehorse.

Once again we were incredibly lucky, because minutes after we took off from base camp, the weather socked in completely. For the next two weeks no aircraft could get anywhere near Mount Logan.

At the hospital, Tim and Peter told us what had happened when their fall down the chute came to a halt. Tim came to a rest on top of the debris covered by a layer of snow, with only one of his boots sticking out, while Peter was hanging down over the edge of a crevasse.

Rescue after the fall.

Peter was conscious and immediately tried to crawl up to help Tim. As he moved, he realized that his leg felt like it was just hanging from his knickers — the bottom part of his leg felt totally loose. He managed to crawl up a ways on one leg, but then found the rope they were attached by was caught deep in the snow and he couldn't pull it up. So he got his Swiss army knife out, managed to open the knife and cut the rope. Then he located Tim lying on his back covered in snow. Peter dug him out immediately. Tim was already turning blue, but Peter was able to resuscitate him. Shortly after that, they hollered up to us on the ridge to say they were okay.

We estimated that they had fallen over 600 vertical metres. They flew most of the way through the air, but when they did make contact with the chute on the way down, it was on cushioning snow rather than rocks. Tim recalled that at one point he was airborne on his back looking up as Peter flew past him. Tim waited for the impact, when he would hit rock or something, but somehow it never came. They made it all the way down without hitting a single thing. That's unbelievable luck.

While Tim and Peter were in the Whitehorse hospital, someone from the Kluane office phoned Jim Sime in Calgary, and Jimmy organized everything. He made arrangements with a Calgary knee specialist who worked with professional sports teams to have a look at Peter's knee, which was badly damaged. Peter was flown there for surgery.

Tim pretty well walked away from the incident, remaining in the Whitehorse hospital for only a couple of days. There was a little bit of skin and muscle missing in various places, but other than that he was fine. When he was ready, I flew home with him.

During my career as a guide or team leader in the mountains, be it with wardens, clients, friends or family, that was the only serious injury accident that occurred. No deaths.

Call it luck, call it faith or whatever, to me the message from the mountains that day was as always — from all of you, we demand respect.

Mount Colin.

12

THE SIDEHILLGOUGER SAYS,

"Blisters on the heels make you walk faster."

IN MY CAREER, I had the opportunity to guide two prime ministers of Canada — Pierre Elliot Trudeau and Jean Chrétien. Trudeau and I climbed three good-sized mountains together and had a lot of laughs in the process.

It all started in the summer of 1977 when Trudeau was in Jasper to attend a meeting. During that time, Trudeau-mania was still in full swing. The wife of his speech writer was a Canadian Alpine Club member, and she suggested that while he was in the Rockies, Trudeau should climb a mountain. It didn't take him long to agree to her suggestion.

On a day I had climbed Mount Colin, I returned home to a message asking me to head over to Jasper Park Lodge to meet with a very important guest. The message didn't include the name of the VIP, but since I had heard rumours about Trudeau being in town, I had a pretty good idea who I was about to meet.

After we were introduced, he told me he would like to climb a mountain. We had a brief talk and I suggested we climb Mount Colin, 2,687 metres, the highest peak in the Colin Range situated just north of the town of Jasper.

Trudeau didn't have any climbing equipment, so to find him some was our next task. It was a Saturday evening and all the stores were closed for the rest of the weekend. We had to improvise. He ended up borrowing my wife's jacket, someone else's climbing knickers, which didn't fit well, and we found him a

pair of boots in the warden storeroom. I even turned my author-
ity over to him for one day. He wore my red socks and I wore the
grey ones. Brown-nosing, they call that.

    Climbers normally walk into the Colin Hut the day before
starting up the mountain, but we didn't have the time. Instead,
we met at the airport the next morning and flew in by helicopter to the base of the mountain.

    Our "team" consisted of Trudeau and a policeman on my
rope, and the speechwriter, his wife, and another guide for the
second rope. The weather was quite poor that morning, so we
stood around for a while hoping it would improve. When it did
get somewhat better, we decided to go ahead with the climb.

Trudeau in red
socks.

Like any good mountaineering story, it all started at the bottom when I tied the rope around Trudeau's chest. He sort of looked at it apprehensively. Then he looked up the ridge and back at me and said, "Willi, I trust you, but what if this rope breaks?"

"Oh, don't worry," I replied. "I have another one at home."

He really liked those kinds of answers, so we got along well from that point on. He had the same kind of sense of humour as I did, and no matter what I said, he had a comeback for it. He got me good a few times, too.

After climbing for a while, we came to a spot where we had to rely on a piton. He looked questionably at this little thing pounded into the rock face. "Are you sure this will hold?"

I said, "Sir, you must have confidence in this equipment. After all, like all government equipment, it is supplied by the lowest bidder."

For his first climb, Trudeau did exceptionally well, but every so often he would have some troubles. I encouraged him by saying things like, "Places like this Mother took me to with the baby buggy." Or "Grandmother would ride her bicycle through here."

All this was taken in good humour. Then we reached the most difficult pitch on the entire ridge. I was straight above Trudeau in a good belay position when he started to climb. For a while it went well, but then things came to a halt. I could hear this scratching and this fuddle-duddle going on down below, and all of a sudden he said, "Willi, I need a helping hand."

I was in a position to pull him up on the rope, but that was neither an ethical choice nor one that he would have appreciated afterward, so I hollered down, "My grandfather always said, 'If you need a helping hand, you will find one at the end of your arm.'"

There was this long, uneasy silence down below from the policeman and the other members of our climbing party. I wasn't quite sure of things any more either. Had I gone too far this time? Then this voice drifts up from the rock face below me and he says, "Willi, I don't think I care for your relatives much."

As we went on, the weather improved. We ended up with quite a good day and traversed the mountain from west to east. Trudeau was quite fit, and even though he was the leader of the country, in a climbing situation he didn't make a move without asking me first. I think that says a lot about his leadership and ability to get things accomplished. He had the confidence to listen to and trust the person who was the expert in a particular field, and for that reason we were able to complete some challenging climbs.

When we reached the top, we took some pictures, then sat down beneath the summit cross for lunch. I had packed a variation of the same lunch I packed every other time I went climbing — a chunk of smoked bacon (known in Austria as *schpeck*), a large hunk of unsliced rye bread, an apple and a knife, all in a plastic bag — and gave it to Trudeau. When I started to eat, he watched what I was doing and did the same. He cut off a slice of *schpeck* and a piece of bread and ate it like that. No sandwich. That's the Austrian way of eating lunch on a mountain. I never liked making sandwiches because they either get soggy or squashed in your pack on the way up. Also, the taste changes as you go higher. Your good sandwich at sea level does not taste the same at 3,000 metres. Later that day, when we were down, Trudeau thanked my wife, Anni, for the nice lunch.

After the climb, we went to Jasper Park Lodge for a beer with the team. It was Sunday though and everything was closed.

There was no beer to be had. Then one of the many policemen who were always around Trudeau said, "Oh, don't worry about it. I'll get you some." A short while later he returned, his police cruiser crammed with every different type of beer imaginable. I wonder where he got that from?

A short break.

As we sat there, drinking our beer, Trudeau asked me what gear he should buy for a future climb. I told him in quite a bit of detail what to buy — the best makes, the features to look for and how to size things properly, for both rock and ice climbing. He just sort of nodded his head, but didn't write anything down. Then we parted ways.

A few years later, Trudeau came back for a second climb, and he invited me out to the Palisades Centre east of Jasper where he was staying. When I arrived, he showed me the gear he had purchased. He had appropriate clothing, boots, crampons, the right type and length of ice axe, and several other pieces of equipment — all exactly as I had recommended. I was amazed that he remembered precisely (and years later) a list of gear that, really, must have been trivial information in his world.

On his second trip, we decided to climb Mount Edith Cavell (3,363 metres). Cavell is a long day's climb, so we had to start really early. Since the Palisades Centre didn't have a restaurant, we decided that the whole team would meet at four o'clock in the morning at the only eating place open in town. There we were the next morning, one policeman, six wardens and I, at the L and W Restaurant, known locally at the time as Greasy Gus's, waiting for Trudeau who was running a little late. The meals were cooked but we didn't want to start eating before the prime minister arrived. The guys were sitting around a table when Trudeau came in.

As you can see,
I took my red
socks back.

I introduced everybody and then I started to carry the meals over to the wardens. Sure enough, Trudeau helped me. He was a pretty good waiter.

As I learned on his first trip to Jasper, Trudeau was always surrounded by several policemen, bodyguards and other people. They would really hen over him, watching his every move. They would tie his shoelaces and fix his collar and constantly ask him if he wanted something. I don't think he liked that, and anyway, I didn't do it, so that's how it worked.

When we went on the Cavell climb, a number of policemen walked with us to the base of the climb. When we started up the mountain, they left. I guess the security I provided him was good enough after that. We climbed Cavell via the East Ridge.

Again, no matter what I said, he had an answer for it. Once I asked him for a job and he said, "What do you have in mind?"

I said, "The department of common sense seems to be understaffed."

He replied, "Oh Willi, you're overqualified."

The two of us moved up the mountain at quite a good pace, both of us well over fifty. At one point, we overtook Jasperite Dwain Wacko and his wife Wendy. I said as we passed, "Make way. The Senior Citizens Express is coming through."

We descended via the normal route off the west side. Once off the mountain, we flew from Verdant Pass to the warden station, which at that time was located at the old fish hatchery. After the dangerous part of the day was over, there were the police again.

Once more, we all wanted to have a beer together. After a climb, we usually headed for the Athabasca beer parlor in town, but because Trudeau was with us, everybody thought we would have to go to some hoity-toity place. I disagreed. Why shouldn't we go to the beer parlor? That's where we always went. So that's where we would go this time as well.

The police wanted Trudeau to ride to town (a distance of about twelve kilometres) in a car they had waiting for him. When we stepped out of the helicopter at the warden station, the fancy black vehicle was parked there with all four doors open, ready to go. Four marked police cars fully equipped with lights and sirens were parked behind it. He looked at all this and said, "Oh, I'll go with Willi," and he jumped into my car.

Those guys were begging, "Oh, Sir. Please, Sir. Please reconsider, Sir." They really wanted him in their car.

I thought to myself, "Well, shit, I have a driver's license. I know how to drive a car."

So I hopped into my car and drove him to town. The policemen all quickly jumped into the four cruisers and followed us. They drove in a row after me, each car spaced two metres behind the one in front of it, all the way into town. Once in Jasper, I couldn't find a parking spot in front of the AthaB (the local name for our destination), so I turned left at the post office and left again into the back alley in order to go around the block. The four police cars followed right behind me, bound and determined not to let me out of their sight. I was thinking to myself, "If I wanted to get rid of the guy, I could have pushed him off a cliff up on the mountain. What do they think I am going to do to him here in the back alley?"

Anyway, out the other side of the alley I came, back out onto the street. Finally, I parked over by the Parks administration building, the four police cars screeching to a halt behind me.

So here we were on the wrong side of the street, in the middle of the block. At any other time I would have jaywalked without a second thought, but with five policemen hovering over us, I wasn't sure if I should coax the prime minister of Canada into breaking the law. This is the kind of situation you don't think about beforehand. So I stood there for a while and Trudeau looked at me and asked, "Well, what?"

I said, "Well, we have to jaywalk here."

And he said, "OK, let's go then," and across he went. So he took me off the hook.

In the AthaB bar, the group of us sat down and ordered some beer. A short while later, a scruffy, aging garbage man missing one of his front teeth approached us. He walked up to Trudeau and said, "I would like to shake the hand of the man who screwed up our country."

The policemen all jumped up, ready for action but Trudeau waved them back. Then he stood up himself, smiled, shook this guy's hand and said, "You look pretty screwed up yourself."

That's Canadian democracy in action. In almost any other country in the world that old guy would have been arrested, or worse.

Again a few years later (1982), Trudeau had a meeting in Banff and asked to go on yet another climb. This request was unplanned, so he had not brought his equipment. I had Peter Fuhrmann fully outfit him and bring him up to Jasper from Banff. Peter then joined us on the climb.

On August 9th, we climbed Mount Athabasca, which is located on the south side of Athabasca Glacier, at the Columbia Icefields. It was Trudeau's first experience with climbing on ice

On top.

and using crampons. He was a bit nervous, but as always, he climbed really well. At that time, he was more than sixty years of age, which tells you something about his fitness level.

Early in the climb, we hit a very steep section. I told him what to do — knees in, ass out and front points of the crampons firmly in the ice. As motivation I promised him that when he made it up to a flat part above, I would tell him a Trudeau joke.

When we reached the flat spot, everyone stood around waiting for me to tell the joke. Before I began, he looked around at the group and said, "I better watch who laughs here now, so I know how many Liberals I have in Alberta."

Actually, it turned out to be more of a Clark joke. You might know it… The country's three leaders were caught by the enemy and were put in front of the firing squad. Trudeau was first up. While he stood there blindfolded, the captain said to his men, "Ready. Aim…" and Trudeau quickly yelled, "AVALANCHE!" Everybody ran for cover and Trudeau disappeared over the hill.

Then it was Broadbent's turn. The captain said, "Ready. Aim…" and Broadbent yelled, "HURRICANE!" Everyone ran for cover and Broadbent disappeared over the hill.

Last up was Clark. As he stood there, he thought to himself, "If it worked for those guys, it is going to work for me too." So the captain said, "Ready. Aim…" and Clark yelled, "FIRE!"

We continued climbing to the top at a good pace. En route, we passed a couple of American parties and when they realized that we had the Canadian prime minister with us, they were really in awe.

On the descent, there was this bergschrund over a crevasse half covered with snow. The lower part was a wide-open gap. Most of the guys leapt across it, but I didn't want Trudeau to in case he didn't jump far enough and fell through, pitched over forward and possibly broke a leg. So I said, "Just sit down and slide down on your ass."

I went first and did it the way I suggested. It wasn't very dignified and Trudeau didn't want to do it that way but I insisted. I knew he wasn't happy about this, but of all the three climbs we had done so far, I felt that this was a place that could really cause us trouble if we weren't careful. Maybe it was my gut feeling at work again. We made it across safely.

I brought Trudeau into my world a few times and in turn,

he invited my family and me into his. Not long after the Colin climb he invited us all to the opening of the parliament in Ottawa. Anni and I got all dressed up and attended a show at the National Arts Centre, during which time we were introduced to the Queen. The next day, the whole family was invited to Trudeau's office. Eva, who was eight, made quite a fuss when we arrived there — she wanted to sit in the prime minister's chair. So Trudeau lifted her into his chair and there she sat, proud as can be.

Over the years we attended several dinners, luncheons and special events with Trudeau. We also met with him at Lake Louise a few times to ski.

On the other hand, I only had the opportunity to climb with Jean Chrétien once. Our day together was enjoyable, but we didn't make the same kind of connection I had with Trudeau. At the time, Chrétien was the Minister of Indian and Northern Affairs, and he had come to Jasper for a meeting with the Chamber of Commerce. Trudeau had told him about the climb he had done on Mount Colin, and Chrétien wanted to try one as well. I decided to start him off on Mount Morro, a peak north of Jasper and also in the Colin Range.

His brother Chichi joined us for the day. Early in the climb, Chrétien wanted to go in one direction but I insisted we go another. At noon he reminded me that he was a cabinet minister and that I was just a government employee, yet there I was continuously telling him which way to go and what to do. I replied, "Listen, you are obviously very capable, otherwise you wouldn't be in the position you are in, but so am I in my own capacity. Right now we are in my environment and I am responsible for getting you up and down this mountain safely."

He didn't challenge me after that on my decisions. In fact, he did very well climbing that mountain. We made it to top and had a nice day, cabinet minister and mountain guide alike.

Jean Chretien.

Virginia Falls,
Nahanni.

13

THE SIDEHILLGOUGER SAYS,

"People who sleep on the side hill

are not on the level."

LIFE HAS NOT BEEN about all work and no play. I was fortunate to spend many fun, relaxing days with my family and friends in the mountains. Every time I was home, either on weekends or in the evenings, Anni, the kids and I always found something interesting to do. We canoed, climbed, bushwhacked to some new place, slept in snow caves, fished in streams seldom visited, and countless other things like that. Often there were a few other kids tagging along as well.

One of our favorite spots was Shalebanks, a relatively unused warden cabin located near the start of the North Boundary Trail. It became like a summer cabin to us, where we had several favourite sites to explore and fish, and where we spent every night around a large open fire. Among our many discoveries there were new fossil beds and natural but perfectly rounded rocks.

Often times we organized longer trips too, like the spring when the whole family travelled the South Boundary Trail of Jasper National Park on cross-country skis. Moving from warden cabin to warden cabin, we completed the 168 kilometre trip in ten days. Eva, our youngest, was nine at the time.

One of the most eventful trips we ever had was on Thanksgiving weekend one year when we rode on horseback into Willow Creek, a warden cabin on the north boundary of the park. During that trip we heard and reported poachers nearby, five-year-old

Eva was pulled into a (very cold) beaver pond by the first large fish she ever hooked, and Susi went on an unintended wild gallop on a horse with only one foot in the stirrup, unable to swing her other leg over the horse's back.

The wildest moment, though, occurred when Anni, Eva and I were relaxing in the cabin on the second morning of our trip. Susi and Fred had gone out to play, and as we later found out, had found an old root cellar dug into the side of a hill near the cabin. Of course they crawled in to explore. Suddenly, they both ran back to the cabin yelling, "Daddy, Daddy, look what we found."

I took a look at what was in their hands and turned white. One of them was holding a rusty hand grenade and the other had

Near the end of the South Boundary trip.

SUSANNA PFISTERER   275

Kayaking.

FACING

The Thelon
River and the
barren lands.

a couple of sticks of dynamite with nitroglycerin crystals covering the bottom ends. It was obvious that the stuff was very old and probably extremely volatile. Aware that the smallest bump could set it off and blow up my family, I was scared. I very carefully took the items from the kids, and then told everyone to get out of the cabin and as far away from me as possible. Slowly, I walked down to the bank of the creek and lobbed them quite a distance away for me, into the water.

We found out a week later after reporting the find that the hand grenade and full box of dynamite had been left in that root cellar by the Lovat Scouts during the Second World War. The ammunition could have very easily exploded while the kids were playing with it. A disposal unit from the army was sent out to Willow Creek to get rid of the stuff and word was that those guys hadn't seen anything that old either, so they were sweating doing that job.

Canoeing and kayaking were both something I really enjoyed when I was home. We spent many enjoyable hours just floating down the river, doing a bit of fishing and soaking up the sun. Day trips were particularly nice because we didn't have to cover a certain amount of ground in a certain period of time. With family and friends we also did some amazing longer trips in places like the Bowron Lakes in BC, and rivers like the Athabasca, Columbia, Yukon and Nahanni. A particularly memorable trip was the six weeks four of us spent on the Thelon River in what is now Nunuvat, crossing the barren lands.

Nahanni National Park in the Northwest Territories was one of the parks that I was responsible for, and although I visited for work, it was actually more of a pleasure than anything. Nahanni is the most beautiful of all the parks, and it is not surprising that it was later named the world's first World Heritage Site. It has the amazing Victoria Falls, followed by a long canyon where the river is actually quite calm and easily paddled. Then there are the natural hot springs, Rabbitkettle (with its tiered calcium mounds) and Grouse, beautiful lakes, a cave system and rare animals such as the Dall sheep. To add to the mystique, several of the park's features have been given names like the Headless Creek, Funeral Range, Deadman Valley, Hell's Gate, Broken Skull River and so on. Clearly, a place to explore.

Once we went to an area called the Blowouts, which are sandstone formations sculpted by the wind. At the time they were outside the borders of the park. It was such an eerie place that our whole group began talking in whispers. When you walked between the bizarrely shaped formations, it felt as if you were walking on top of something — as if it were hollow underneath.

Also outside of the original park boundaries, but now included, are the mountains, named the Cirque of the Unclimbables. These granite spires are similar to the Bugaboos but maybe even steeper. In spite of the area's name, mountaineers had been in there prior to the establishment of the park and had climbed most of the peaks, naming them some really fancy names like the Lotus Flower Tower.

The Nahanni wardens and I did some rescue practices in the Cirque of the Unclimbables, but I was never involved in a rescue in that area. The wardens, of course, did a few, but in that part of the country they were more likely to be called to a river rescue.

Deep-snow school in Rogers Pass was my reward to the wardens who had worked really hard all year long, training and carrying out rescues. I would invite the ones who had taken part in all the training sessions and the ones who had carried out the sometimes risky rescues. With its unusually high snowfalls, deep-snow skiing on Mount Fidelity was terrific and we always had a lot of fun. We had a snowcat that serviced the weather station at Mount Fidelity to haul us up the mountain and we had places to stay, so the only real cost of this school was fuel. I applied seventeen times to the higher-ups to run that school and seventeen times they didn't approve it. Seventeen times we went anyway.

We would always ski in pairs at the Pass. It was necessary to stick together because there were too many things that could happen, such as falling down a tree well, which required immediate help. I always paired up with Gord Peyto because he knew the area really well and he was one of the best skiers.

Mount Fidelity had several great runs, featuring both tree skiing and open slopes. The Bostock Headwall, the Mine Run (watch out for the old mine shafts) and the South Run were all great, but my personal favourite was the Windfalls where numerous huge BC trees had fallen perpendicular to the hill, and in the winter were covered with several feet of snow. If you knew where to ski, the effect was like going down a staircase — two turns and a drop, two turns and a drop. If you didn't know where to ski, things could get dicey.

The trick was to always get down first in the untracked snow because it was much more difficult to ski on tracked terrain. Gordy and I knew all the best routes, but the rest of the guys soon became wise to us, so we had to use some creative tactics to get the best snow. We would stop in a place where they couldn't see the slope below, for example, making it impossible for them to choose a route. Then I would say, "Okay, we are going to go to the left down here."

With wardens on horseback.

Everybody skied off to the left while Gordy and I headed right. On the next run, Gordy would say, "Okay, we are going to the left again." Wise to us, everybody went to the right, while Gordy and I skied the best snow to the left. That wasn't going to work a second time, so the next run, I said, "Okay, Gordy, you go to the left and I'll go to the right." We knew that behind a little clump of trees on the South Run just below us was a perfect open slope of snow. So Gordy took off to the left with everybody following right on his heals. Meanwhile, I headed straight down into the open draw. Gordy let the other wardens pass him by, made a sharp right turn and came into the draw just below me. I didn't see him coming and we crashed... the two of us on that wide-open slope and we hit each other. Oh boy.

The hundredth anniversary of Canadian National Parks in 1985 was cause for celebration for all of us, and we marked the year with a few great trips. That summer, a group of us spent some time in Banff National Park, Canada's first national park and thus the reason for the anniversary, and climbed eleven first ascents, all in one small area of the park. This was odd because at the time it would have been impossible to find eleven first ascents in all of Jasper Park, but Banff had tended to be more about the sights and mountains accessible via the highway corridor, rather than deep in the backcountry.

I had thought for a long time that it would be nice to spend New Year's on top of Mount Edith Cavell, a mountain that holds so many good memories for me. As the hundredth anniversary of Canadian National Parks approached in 1985, I thought what better way to start that year off.

I sent out a notice to the wardens in all the mountain national parks, asking who wanted to participate in the New Year's climb. There were numerous applications, but in the end we went with three teams of three. Six wardens representing five national parks took part, while the third team was composed of Susi, Fredy and me.

A couple of weeks before the climb, a helicopter was in the area doing a different job for the park, so I had it fly some wood up to the top of the mountain which we could use at New Year's to make a fire.

The problem was that in the days leading up to New Year's that year, a major cold spell descended on the Jasper area. My thermometer had run off the scale at −40°c and the wind chill dropped into the −50s. As we started up the mountain, the temperatures improved slightly due to an inversion. The Jasper Snowmobile Club came out in that weather and hauled us fifteen kilometres up the Cavell road (which was closed to traffic and unplowed in the winter) to the bottom of the mountain. We then skied around the base of the mountain to Verdant Pass, set up our tents and slept there.

The next day at 9:00 a.m., when the winter darkness had dispelled, we went for the summit. It took all day. We had to climb on the south ridge of the neighbouring peak to its east summit, then climb down onto the west ridge of Cavell to avoid the large avalanche slope on the west face.

It was windy and cold, still in the −30s up there. The climbing was straightforward with the exception of the summit buttress where we had to cut steps in the ice and belay each other carefully. After seven hours of climbing, we arrived at the summit cross at 4:00 p.m., not long before darkness descended again.

The first thing we did when we got there was to pull the summit register out of the cairn and write "Happy Birthday, Parks Canada." With smiling faces and a quick handshake we congratulated each other and then it was back to work — the work of love, called survival.

We built some snow shelters, which was difficult because there was only poor-quality snow with ice underneath. In the end, the housing was not up to national park's standards, but lucky for us, there was no inspection.

In the meantime, it grew dark and heavy clouds moved in from the west. Our plan was to shoot off some flares at 7:30 p.m. to coincide with the town fireworks, and then at midnight to light the fire, but we feared that the clouds from the west would engulf

On our way up.

the mountain and we would be lost in obscurity. Also, for us to get out of our sleeping bags, dress fully in the dark in extreme cold and blizzard conditions to light a fire at midnight could have been a critical mistake, possibly with some terrible consequences. So we lit the fire and shot off all the flares at 7:30 instead. The flares went up in the air and as soon as the wind from the north face hit them, they flew back behind us so people in town did not actually see them. Those that were looking at that time did see the fire, however. As our group sat up there on the peak beside the roaring fire, we all enjoyed some well-chilled rum.

Since I had written a notice in the local newspaper the week before, stating that at midnight we would light the fire up on Cavell, many people in town kissed each other at the stroke of 12 o'clock and then rushed outside to look up at the peak. Sadly, they were disappointed that there was no light on the summit at midnight, as promised, but there was nothing we could do. We were only role players: the mountain was the conductor and a storm had the final say. We really appreciated the interest and support we received for our project though.

So that evening we crawled into our humble abodes, pulled the sleeping bags over our heads and tried to stay warm. During the night the wind shifted to the west, which exposed our three snow-house hamlet to a full-force blizzard, but we didn't know how strong the wind really was blowing until the next morning when we climbed back onto the summit ridge and started travelling across it. We literally had to crawl across the metre and a half wide ridge on our hands and knees for fear of being blown off the mountain by the hundred kilometre an hour winds. From there, one belay and one long rappel got us off the summit buttress.

Then we followed our approach route back to the Verdant Pass camp and to our trusty skis.

As we moved downwards, the temperature again began to drop (moving from the −30s back into the −40s with even higher wind chills). When we reached the head of the Astoria trail, there were ten snowmobiles waiting for us, our friends from the Jasper Snowmobile Club. They had come to help us down, which we really appreciated, especially since they had waited for us for some time in those bone chilling temperatures. They hauled us and our equipment down to the highway and gave us a ride back to Jasper. Their neighbourly helpfulness was warmly accepted and underlined the reason for this entire project — a gesture of appreciation.

Spending New Year's Eve 1985 on top of Mount Edith Cavell was a very cool experience.

Sunset over the
mountains.

14

THE SIDEHILLGOUGER SAYS,

"In mountain rescue work there are no heroes,

just teammates."

THROUGHOUT MY TIME in the mountains, I had the feeling that one day my luck would run out. I accepted that feeling as part of the life I led and the amazing joy the mountains had given me. After so many close calls and near misses, it seemed almost a given that one day I would get badly hurt or possibly killed while climbing, or maybe a rescue would go terribly wrong.

In the end, what did happen was completely unanticipated and far, far worse than anything I could have imagined for my family and me. On March 23, 1987, my son Fredy died in an avalanche accident in Blue River, British Columbia. He was twenty-four years old.

After leading or participating in more than seven hundred rescues during my career, the very last time I was called out before I retired, all I could do was close the eyes of my own son.

I found out about the accident just before noon that day when a call came into the Parks office in Jasper. The reporting person informed us that several heli-skiers were caught in a large avalanche in Blue River, two hundred kilometres west of Jasper. Since Fred worked as a heli-ski guide in that area, I was immediately alert.

I asked the chief warden if I could take the dog master, the search dog and some wardens to go and help out. Blue River is a two-hour drive from Jasper, outside the national park system, but we had done work in the area before so this wasn't an unusual request. He said no. I rounded up some wardens and the dog master and went anyway.

We drove halfway, to the town of Valemount, where we met with the police who had more information. They told us that seven people had been caught in the slide. Since all the skiers had avalanche beacons on, they had already been found and dug out of the snow. None had survived. I asked if a guide was among them and they said no.

Somehow, though, I already knew his information wasn't correct. I had a gut feeling that Fred was involved but I didn't say anything. I told the wardens and dog master to take the equipment and go back to Jasper. I drove a few miles to Tete Jaune Cache where I had a small piece of land, and I checked on the two cows I had there. In doing that, I think I was avoiding the news that I was pretty sure was coming my way. After some time, I returned to my car and headed to Blue River.

Fred.

When I walked into the heli-ski operation office in Blue River, the first person I saw was the sister of Fred's girlfriend, Liana. Theresa, who was employed at the resort, didn't have to say a word. I knew immediately by the look on her face that my worst fears were true. A short while later, a policeman, who I knew well, had to officially tell me that my son was dead. He could only get halfway through the news before he broke down.

I was told Fred, a lead guide for the operation, and his group of ten skiers were the first to be flown to the top of an unskied slope after a short rest break. He needed to do a snow profile to see if the slope was safe to ski on, so he left his group in a safe spot near the helicopter landing pad and asked them to stay there. He skied into the slope a ways, removed his skis and started to dig a pit, following the standard method of assessing the snowpack. In the meantime, the helicopter flew down to get another load of people and bring them up to the same landing pad. As the helicopter approached to land, Fred's group moved over a ways in order to avoid the wind and blades of the machine. Simultaneously, a fracture line started to develop a distance above them on the mountainside. The entire mountain let go. Fred, who was still in the middle of the slope with his skis off, didn't stand a chance. Six members of his group were sucked into the edge of the slide.

By the time I arrived, the bodies had been recovered and all I could do was identify my son. He was just lying there with his eyes open and a really angry look on his face.

I would have given anything to trade places with him right then and there. I had led my life. It had been a great life in so many ways, but a difficult one at times, too. Nothing compared to this though. I had had so many close calls and beaten the odds so many times; I just felt that this time it should have been me. It was so completely unfair. Fred was just barely starting out and he had such a joy for life.

He was a smart kid, but like me, not suited for academic situations. He just didn't like to go to school, but he made up for that with an active life. And he sure did a good job of that.

Fred had so much enthusiasm for skiing, kayaking, flying planes, climbing, travelling and so many other things. Having passed several guiding exams, he was on his way to becoming a fully certified mountain guide.

Fred was very friendly and had a gentle, caring side to him. He had so many good friends and people who loved him. Even strangers were drawn to him. Blue River was a great place for him because it didn't matter if you were rich and famous like many of the guests, or the salt of the earth like the townspeople. He could pick up a conversation with anyone, anytime. We used to joke that if some guy ever held him at gunpoint, Fred would have made friends with him and had him laughing within five minutes.

SUSANNA PFISTERER   291

After the accident, Anni and I questioned ourselves. Were we right to introduce our kids to the mountains? Fred was following in my footsteps and it cost him his life. Maybe we should have insisted that he go to university instead.

Some people, including the media, asked the standard questions like why did you let him do such a dangerous job or why would anyone heli-ski knowing the risks?

In the early days, we did have moments of blaming ourselves, but neither Anni nor I believed in caging our kids to keep them safe. That's not living. Fred only lived for twenty-four years, but they were a full twenty-four years.

And he loved his job at Blue River. Every day he would jump out of bed and say, "Yahoo, I get to go skiing again today." Even in hindsight, we would not have kept him from the mountains or prevented him from doing his job. Certainly, if somehow we could have prevented the accident, we would have, but we would not have kept him from doing what he loved. Fred did his job and he did it with honour, and the mountain took his life. That's where he wanted to be—in the mountains. He died *truly* living.

Before the accident occurred, I strongly believed that when your time is up, your time is up. If this is your day, you are going to die no matter what you do. I can tell you one story after another where people did everything wrong in the mountains and got away with it, while others did everything right except one small thing, or just had really bad luck, and died.

I noticed this with some of the well-known mountaineers of Europe. One guy had climbed many very difficult routes in Europe and Asia. He died when he slipped off the toilet seat he had been standing on at home and hit his head on the sink.

He had been trying to change a light bulb. Another famous climber died when he backed over a small cliff while playing frisbee with his family at a picnic site.

It took a while for me after Fred's death to think that way again, but I eventually I did. He just did not have as much luck as I had. He had a terrific life during the short period that he lived and he packed in so much fun and adventure, but he simply did not have luck on his side.

Fred's accident marked the end of my career. I retired a month later. I had felt the end drawing near in the few years before Fred's death. When I was young and on top of my game, I would stick to my guns, but as I got older I mellowed somewhat. Then accidents started to happen — the big one on Logan and a few minor ones, too. I felt that my role as leader was shifting and I wasn't fully in charge anymore.

Lawyers and lawsuits were becoming much more prominent in the eighties, so I hesitated doing things the way I always had in the past. Parks Canada lawyers told me that if I had trouble, I was on my own. They could not back me up. I would have been hung out to dry if I had lost a warden in a training or rescue situation. When you start thinking about things like that, it is time to quit.

I sort of decided that the whole job was like competitive sports. You had to be in top shape; otherwise you were a liability. If you were a leader then you had to be in better shape than everybody else. I found that as I got older, the mountains became higher, the packs heavier and the cold colder. Eventually, it was time to quit and hand the whole thing over to a younger crew. And by that point, there were enough young wardens who really knew what they were doing. They were ready to take over. Besides,

I had too much respect for the mountains to crawl my way up, huffing and puffing and spitting.

I am very proud of what we accomplished as a team in the warden service in the arenas of public safety and mountain rescue. When I started out, the average warden was about as knowledgeable about mountaineering and the mountains as an Alpine Club member in Edmonton. When I left the job twenty-three years later, there were six fully qualified mountain guides in the warden service, and the average warden was almost as knowledgeable and capable as a certified assistant guide. Wardens still patrolled the valleys on horseback, but now they were as handy with a carabiner and a piton as they were a halter and saddle.

In the beginning, everything was improvised. We had the simplest of equipment. Over the years, through innovation and continuously updated techniques, rescue response times were reduced from days to hours.

We prevented numerous deaths by setting up preventative systems like avalanche control and by educating people in safe mountain travel.

We trained hard, in the worst of conditions. I would purposely plan trips like the Eight Pass Route on the coldest days or in the highest avalanche hazard. This way, if we received a call for help, we could respond regardless of temperature and hazard. It was part of the job, and to be ready for any type of rescue situation, we had to go out there and experience it firsthand.

I admit I was afraid at times, but I believe that a healthy dose of fear keeps you alive.

I chose a long, hazardous and demanding route in life, but it has been a most satisfying one. I never shied away from the steep,

the unstable or the cold. The wardens and I had our fair share of great moments and also some very close calls, many beyond our control. In all those years, during all those practices and rescues and climbs, naturally there were times when things took on a life of their own, for better or for worse. Regardless, I never asked a warden to do something I wouldn't do myself.

Over the years, I travelled with so many people, some of them hundreds of times. We stood on high peaks, crossed glaciers, skied fresh powder, paddled amazing waterways. Most of the people I travelled with have not been mentioned by name in this book. As I stated earlier, the best stories result from situations that are out of the ordinary — funny, odd, scary, tragic. The vast majority of trips went as planned and were wonderful, but did not necessarily make for a good story. All of them remain great memories though. For me, every person, every mountain, and every creek is a memory of some sort and no one can take those memories away.

LEFT
Some of the
people I had
to work with!
Fred and Susi at
Rogers Pass
RIGHT
Skiing with Eva.

As for the future of public safety and mountain rescue, I believe that we constructed a solid program with a strong foundation and a strong framework. As time moves on, there will be changes and improvements to the framework, but my hope is the foundation will remain strong.

I would like to thank all those I worked with for letting me be a member of the team. It was an honour and a privilege.

As for me personally, I came to Canada in search of adventure and found so much more. Canada is such an amazing country and I was lucky enough to see a lot of it — the awe-inspiring mountains of British Columbia and Alberta, the west coast, the north, some of its great rivers like the Thelon, the Yukon, the Athabasca/Mackenzie, and places of astounding beauty like the Nahanni and the barren lands. So many mountaineers think that the mountains are somehow more exotic and challenging in other countries. I guess I thought the same when I came from the Austrian Alps to Canada. By all means, climb mountains around the world, but don't forget the amazing ones we have in our own backyard. I am so proud to have called Canada home.

It is likely that more Canadians have seen a rhino in the wild than a musk ox, which I think is unfortunate. I urge people to explore more of Canada. There are countless, diverse natural wonders to discover.

In this journey of life, my family and I travelled a long ways together. We shared some great moments and some terrible defeats.

I could not have done the job I did or celebrated the successes without the love and support of Anni. She was an amazing

wife, mother, business woman and friend who had a love for the mountains, travel, art, books and people. She and I had our difficulties in the end, but I was grateful for all the wonderful times we had together and the family we raised. We lost Anni in 1995, far too early. Susi and Eva are with me still and have given me four wonderful grandchildren, the joys of my later life.

Well, that's my story. So now what are you waiting for? Quit sitting there on the couch, sucking back that coffee, and go spend a little time of your own on the sidehill. The memories will last you a lifetime.

GLOSSARY OF TERMS

Alpine terrain: high, barren mountain landscape with little or no vegetation above the tree line.

Avalanche: the fall of a mass of snow or ice down the slope of a mountain. Does not apply to rock.

Belaying: the paying out of a rope tied to a climber and running around the body of a belayer or around a tree, rock, or through a snap link. This term also includes the application of braking action on a rope by the belayer in order to prevent a dangerous fall by the climber.

Belay point: the point selected and used by the belayer from which he can best protect a climber and himself from a fall. It can also refer to a tree, rock, piton or other object to which a rope may be tied for the purpose of belaying.

Bergschrund: a large crevasse which separates the moving ice of a glacier from the anchored ice of the mountain mass.

Chimney: a vertical fissure in a rock large enough to accommodate the body of a climber.

Chute: a chute-like fissure in the rock caused by erosion or glacial action. It may be vertical or sloping and is generally wider than a chimney.

Climbing rope: a nylon rope used as a safety measure. It is 36.5 metres in length, 1.1 centimetre in diameter, has a 1,800 kilogram tensile strength and some elasticity.

Continuous climbing: when all members of a roped climbing party move simultaneously.

Cornice: a mass of snow overhanging the leeward side of a ridge.

Crack: a fissure in the rock only large enough to introduce fingers, feet, arms, legs or pitons.

Crampons: hinged metal frames, which may be attached to shoes or boots and from which spikes project downwards/ forward to facilitate walking/climbing on ice or hard snow.

Crevasse: a fissure in the surface of a glacier caused by strains incident to the motion of the ice.

Escarpment: a long outcropping or cliff, extending several kilometres.

Exposed climb: a climb from which a fall would be dangerous or fatal.

Face of rock: the sheer unbroken front of a cliff or a rock.

Fixed rope: a rope which is securely tied or belayed, usually at the top of a steep slope or cliff.

Free climbing: climbing without the aid of ropes.

Front pointing: using the front points of crampons to climb ice slopes of an angle of more than forty-five degrees.

Glaciers: large, slow moving masses of ice and snow in the valleys of high mountains.

Glissading: descending a slope of hard packed snow by sliding in a sitting or standing position.

Gully: a shallow ravine caused by erosion.

Hold: a support of rock, snow or ice used by the feet or hands in progressing from one position to another. It also refers to the method of using these supports.

Ice axe: an instrument similar to a pick, consisting of a wooden (now plastic) shaft, and metal adze, pick and ferrule, intended primarily for cutting holds in snow and ice, as an aid for balance and in probing for concealed crevasses.

Icefall: the portion of a glacier in which the surface ice is broken into a mass of blocks and crevasses due to an abrupt change in gradient of the bed of the glacier. It occurs when the glacier falls over steep terrain. The term does not apply to falling ice. (see avalanche)

Igneous rock: rock formed through heat; metal-bearing rock.

Margin of safety: the protective buffer a climber keeps between what he knows to be the limit of his ability and what he actually climbs.

Moraine: the accumulation of rock debris carried on or deposited by the glacier. Lateral moraines are found on either side of a glacier. Medial moraines are found in the centre and terminal moraines are deposited at the front of the glacier.

Mountains, new: high, rough jagged peaks with little evidence of wind or water erosion.

Mountains, old: rounded, forested, rolling type of mountains with no precipitous peaks.

Pitch: a steep and difficult part of a mountain where it is impractical or impossible to stop for a rest.

Piton: a steel spike used as an aid in climbing. It is hammered into ice or cracks in the rock and serves as a belay point.

Piton hammer: a short light hammer used for driving pitons. It has a wooden handle and the head comes to a sharp point, which is used primarily for clearing debris from cracks and chopping ice off holds to be used.

Rappel: the process whereby a climber lowers himself by means of a rope down steep rock, snow or ice.

Rappel point: the rock, tree or rope sling to which the rappel rope is secured.

Rockfall: the fall of any quantity of rock on a mountainside.

Scree slope: steep slope composed of small, unconsolidated rocks and gravel that will roll under foot.

Self arrest: the skill of stopping yourself using an ice axe, following a fall on steep snow.

Seracs: large blocks of ice formed in places where crevasses become extremely numerous and convoluted.

Sidehillgouger: A folkloric creature with two legs on one side of its body much shorter than the other two, making it well adapted for a life of grazing on the tender grasses of steep mountain slopes. Since the sidehillgouger can move in only one direction, over time it forms an endless circular gouged-out path.

Sound rock: firm rock that holds together well; the opposite of rotten rock.

Snaplink/carabiner: an oval-shaped metal ring with a hinged gate to permit fastening it to a rope or piton.

Talus slope: a slope composed of debris fallen from a dominating rock face. The steepness of talus slopes may vary from about twenty-five degrees for fine debris to about forty-five for coarse material.

Tension climbing: climbing in which the belayer holds the climber on the rock with tension on the rope.

Traversing: climbing across or zigzagging, rather than climbing directly up or down.

Wall: a vertical or nearly vertical mountainside.

My grandchildren
from the left,
Sophie, Teslyn,
Erica and Lukas

ACKNOWLEDGEMENTS

Fifty Percent of Mountaineering is Uphill has been a labour of love — a way to remember and honour my dad, mom and brother. It has taken years to complete and bring to publication, a process that has been very cathartic for me. However, without the help, support and guidance of many people, the project would never have come into being. I cannot begin to express my gratitude to all of these individuals.

I wanted the book to be about my father's memories rather than people's memories of him, so I did not interview others. I did, however, gather and use interviews that others did with Dad. One of the most interesting and useful of these was done by Vikki Wallace for the Jasper Yellowhead Museum and Archives. Thank you Vikki for your wonderful work, the museum for letting me use it, and Megan Follows for accessing it for me.

Another helpful interview was done by Peter Amman. Thank you Peter.

During his time as alpine specialist, my father gave slide shows a few times a year in different venues, to tell people about the mountain rescue program and to educate them about mountain safety. These entertaining lectures (as he called them) were well received. For that reason, Dad and I decided very early on that the book format would be similar to the lecture format — photos and stories: some funny, some sad, some triumphant, some cautionary, with a strong underlying message about safety in the mountains. After an extensive search, I was able to find a VHS tape of one of these talks, which has been invaluable. Thank you so much to the Parks Canada staff in Jasper who helped locate the tape, as well as to the staff in other parks offices who spent the time to look.

My dad passed away somewhat unexpectedly on July 21, 2010 at the age of eighty-three. To that point we had taped many of his stories, as well as gathered interviews, reports, newspaper articles, and other material. We had an outline and a rough draft of the first two chapters but not much else. Dad tended to be very sparse on the details when he told a story, but often I had two or three versions of the same narrative from different sources, which I was then able to patch together.

During the writing process (largely after my dad's death), I made every effort to follow up and double-check all of the technical and geographical details of the book. It is important to note that if errors remain, they are mine, not his. Friends and colleagues of Dad's often helped me understand or advised me on these technical, geographical or missing details. Thank you Gerry Israelson, Clair Israelson, Joe Couture and a number of others for your help with my questions.

After Dad's formal funeral, many people gathered on a beautiful warm July day at the Parks barns in Jasper to tell stories about Dad and the mountains. These were taped. Thank you so much to Kelly Deagle and the warden office staff for doing this for us. Thank you also, to all the people who talked that day. Again I used this tape to fill in details.

Several authors gave me support and answered my questions as I worked on this project. In particular, I would like to thank Sid Marty for taking the time to read some of my chapters early on and give me valuable advice on how to proceed.

Kathy Calvert and Dale Portman were only a phone call away when I needed support, information or advice. I so appreciate everything both of you have done for me.

Finally thank you to Edmonton author, Todd Babiak for taking a couple of hours away from your family holiday weekend to talk to me.

I tend to be somewhat technologically challenged and would like to thank Roger Gruys for helping me out with my computer issues at a key moment in time.

Thank you Richard Ireland for the advice you gave me when I was unsure how to proceed.

Almost all of the photos in the book are Dad's or family photos, with a few exceptions. The cover photo, taken by Harry Rowed, was commissioned by Dad for Willi's Ski Shop. Thank you to the Rowed family and the Allen family (who now own many of Harry Rowed's photos) for the use of the head shot.

Many of the photos of the 1959 Logan climb were lost at the end of the trip. Those remaining were shared among the group. It has been difficult to ascertain who took which photo, but individual shots were taken either by Hans Gmoser, Phillippe Delesalle or Karl Richer. Thank you for these wonderful pictures. Hans Gmoser made a film about the climb, which was wonderful to watch and filled in a number of details for me. Many thanks.

Helen Rolfe, a professional editor and writer, spent many hours doing the initial edit of the book. She understood how much I wanted to clean up the text while still keeping all of Dad's unique ways of expressing himself intact. My deepest gratitude, Helen, for all your help.

Paul Matwychuk, the general manager at NeWest Press in Edmonton, phoned one exciting day to say that the Press would like to publish Dad's story. Thank you so much Paul and the editorial board at NeWest for believing in the project.

Editor Anne Nothof has worked with me to get the book ready for publication. It has been a pleasure working with you, Anne. I so appreciate your editing work, but also your patience and support in answering my repeated questions about other parts of the process.

A huge thank you goes to Matt Bowes, marketing and production coordinator at NeWest Press, for working so hard on producing and getting the book out there.

Natalie Olsen spent hours making dusty, damaged, old photographs and slides look great, and then skillfully integrated them into the text. Thank you so much, Natalie.

Although I kept the project quiet for a long time, several friends have given me encouragement as the book neared completion. I am so appreciative.

My sister Eva supported me throughout the years, in several ways, which I am truly grateful for. Thank you Eva for reading the text and giving me your input.

My daughters, Sophie and Teslyn, have been there throughout the writing and editing process, experiencing the fun and frustrations with me. I love you both so much.

From my perspective, this is also a book about my mom and brother, both of whom have left us much too soon. My mom deserves a tremendous amount of credit in what Dad accomplished. She was often a single mother of three young kids when he was away for weeks. She supported him in so many ways, and an adventuress herself, joined him when she could. Thank you Mom, from all of us.

Finally, I want to thank my dad from the bottom of my heart. These are his stories and his life. I have had the privilege of putting the stories together in book form for him.

During his life, my father never really searched out recognition or publicity for himself. Even in situations where he was presented with an award, my sister and I had difficulty getting him to attend the function. It is telling, for example, that in the summit logs at the top of mountains, while others wrote pages, he would simply write the date and "Willi." His drive instead was just to be outside, in the mountains — that was where he was the happiest.

In the years following his retirement, numerous people asked Dad if he would write his memoirs, and a couple of authors asked if they could do it for him. He always declined, saying that he didn't think his story would be of much interest to anyone other than a few older park wardens. By 2006, however, he was the grandfather of three very young children with one soon to follow. At that point, I asked him if I could write his story for him as a gift to his grandchildren. He agreed.

Once we got started, I believe he really enjoyed it. Telling the stories momentarily seemed to ease the chronic pain he was living with. We spent many hours taping his memories, with me constantly asking him questions and keeping him (somewhat) on track. We did particularly well on the three-hour drives back and forth from Golden BC, the home of my sister, while my young daughters slept in their car seats behind us. He would stare out the window at the mountains of the Icefields Parkway and remember stories about so many of them. Before he passed away he knew that I wanted try to publish the book and he was in agreement. This is for you, Dad.